Jesse Lyman Hurlbut

Imperial songs

For Sunday schools, social meetings, Epworth leagues, revival services

Jesse Lyman Hurlbut

Imperial songs
For Sunday schools, social meetings, Epworth leagues, revival services

ISBN/EAN: 9783337266493

Printed in Europe, USA, Canada, Australia, Japan

Cover: Foto ©Thomas Meinert / pixelio.de

More available books at **www.hansebooks.com**

FOR

Sunday Schools, Social Meetings
Epworth Leagues, Revival Services

JESSE L. HURLBUT, D.D., STEPHEN V. R. FORD

EDITORS

NEW YORK: HUNT & EATON
CINCINNATI: CRANSTON & CURTS

Electrotyping, printing, and binding by
HUNT & EATON,
150 Fifth Avenue, New York.

PREFACE.

THE songs of a people enter into their life, and shape their character to such a degree that he spoke wisely who said, "Let me but make the songs of a nation, and I care not who may make its laws." It may be said in our time that the songs in our Sunday schools, sung by ten millions of young people, are forming the Church of the future not less but perhaps more than the lessons that are studied.

Therefore the songs of the Sunday school should be thoughtfully chosen. They should be more than popular melodies and simple rhymes. They should utter noble thoughts in right words; they should possess gospel truth and spiritual power. The singing of the Sunday school should be a part of its educational work, while it imparts an atmosphere of gladness to its services. It should inspire an intelligent as well as an ardent piety. It should refine and not lower the taste of those who join in the singing.

With such aims this book has been prepared. The work of selection and composition has been done mainly by Mr. Stephen V. R. Ford, but the Editor of the Sunday school department has carefully examined the words of each song, and Mr. A. S. Newman, of New York, has reviewed the music. Thanks are due to C. C. Converse, author of the popular song, "What a Friend we have in Jesus;" to Fanny J. Crosby, the popular hymn writer; Mrs. Joseph F. Knapp, whose "Blessed Assurance" is sung in all lands; Drs. Philip Phillips and H. R. Palmer; G. Froelich, John Hyatt Brewer, Frank Treat Southwick, H. P. Danks, Rev. Samuel Alman, William G. Fischer, Will L. Thompson, Rev. E. S. Lorenz, Rev. Robert Lowry, R. E. Hudson, Rev. A. C. Ferguson, and others, for their kindness in permitting the use of their songs.

JESSE L. HURLBUT.
STEPHEN V. R. FORD.

DEVOTIONAL READINGS

FOR

SUNDAY SCHOOLS AND SOCIAL MEETINGS.

I. Praise.

Leader. I will bless the Lord at all times: his praise shall continually be in my mouth.

School. My soul shall make her boast in the Lord; the humble shall hear thereof and be glad.

O magnify the Lord with me, and let us exalt his name together!

Bless the Lord, O my soul: and all that is within me, bless his holy name.

Bless the Lord, O my soul, and forget not all his benefits;

Who forgiveth all thine iniquities; who healeth all thy diseases:

Who redeemeth thy life from destruction; who crowneth thee with loving kindness and tender mercies;

Who satisfieth thy mouth with good things; so that thy youth is renewed like the eagle's.

Bless the Lord, ye his angels, that excel in strength, that do his commandments, hearkening unto the voice of his word.

Bless ye the Lord, all ye his hosts; ye ministers of his, that do his pleasure.

Bless the Lord, all his works in all places of his dominion; bless the Lord, O my soul.

Praise waiteth for thee, O God, in Zion: and unto thee shall the vow be performed.

Rejoice evermore.

Pray without ceasing.

In everything give thanks: for this is the will of God in Christ Jesus concerning you.

Praise ye the Lord. Praise, O ye servants of the Lord, praise the name of the Lord.

Blessed be the name of the Lord from this time forth and for evermore.

From the rising of the sun unto the going down of the same the Lord's name is to be praised.

Praise ye the Lord. I will praise the Lord with my whole heart, in the assembly of the upright, and in the congregation.

Praise ye the Lord. Praise ye the name of the Lord; praise him, O ye servants of the Lord.

Ye that stand in the house of the Lord, in the courts of the house of our God,

Praise the Lord; for the Lord is good: sing praises unto his name; for it is pleasant.

Additional: Psalms 148 and 150.

Gloria, 98.

Hymns: 7, 12, 18, 31, 56, 62, 64, 80, 90, 91, 103, 104, 156, 163, 170.

II. Prayer.

O magnify the Lord with me, and let us exalt his name together.

O come, let us worship and bow down; let us kneel before the Lord our Maker.

Lord God of Israel, there is no God like thee, in heaven above, or on earth beneath, who keepest covenant and mercy with thy servants that walk before thee with all their heart:

Have thou respect unto the prayer of thy servant, and to his supplication, O Lord my God, to hearken unto the cry and to the prayer, which thy servant prayeth before thee to-day:

That thine eyes may be open toward this house night and day, even toward the place of which thou hast said, My name shall be there: that thou mayest hearken unto the prayer which thy servant shall make toward this place.

And hearken thou to the supplication of thy servant, and of thy people Israel, when they shall pray toward this place: and hear thou in heaven thy dwelling-place: and when thou hearest, forgive.

For the eyes of the Lord are upon the righteous, and his ears are open unto their cry; The face of the Lord is against them that do evil.

Call unto me, and I will answer thee, and show thee great and mighty things, which thou knowest not.

4

I sought the Lord, and he heard me and delivered me from all my fears.

Delight thyself in the Lord, and he shall give thee the desires of thine heart

He spake a parable unto them to this end, that men ought always to pray and not to faint.

Praying always with all prayer and supplication in the Spirit, and watching thereunto with all perseverance and supplication for all saints.

The Lord is nigh unto all them that call upon him, to all that call upon him in truth.

He will fulfill the desire of them that fear him: he also will hear their cry, and will save them.

Call upon me in the day of trouble: I will deliver thee, and thou shalt glorify me.

If I regard iniquity in my heart, the Lord will not hear me:

But verily God hath heard me; he hath attended to the voice of my prayer.

After this manner therefore pray ye: Our Father which art in heaven, Hallowed be thy name.

Thy kingdom come. Thy will be done in earth, as it is in heaven.

Give us this day our daily bread.

And forgive us our debts, as we forgive our debtors.

And lead us not into temptation, but deliver us from evil: For thine is the kingdom, and the power, and the glory, forever. Amen.

Additional: Matt. 7. 7–11; Psalm 123; 1 John 3. 22; Heb. 10. 22; James 1. 5–7; Psalm 40. 1–3.

Hymns: 35, 53, 111, 113, 150, 155, 168, 171, 180, 185, 188, 198, 201, 203, 209, 211.

III. The Church.

The Lord loveth the gates of Zion more than all the dwellings of Jacob.

Do good in thy good pleasure unto Zion: build thou the walls of Jerusalem.

If I forget thee. O Jerusalem, let my right hand forget her cunning.

If I do not remember thee, let my tongue cleave to the roof of my mouth; if I prefer not Jerusalem above my chief joy.

I have set watchmen upon thy walls, O Jerusalem, which shall never hold their peace day nor night: ye that make mention of the Lord, keep not silence,

And give him no rest, till he establish, and till he make Jerusalem a praise in the earth.

They that trust in the Lord shall be as mount Zion, which cannot be removed, but abideth forever.

As the mountains are round about Jerusalem, so the Lord is round about his people from henceforth even forever.

The church of the living God, the pillar and ground of the truth.

Now therefore ye are no more strangers and foreigners, but fellow citizens with the saints, and of the household of God;

And are built upon the foundation of the apostles and prophets, Jesus Christ himself being the chief corner stone;

In whom all the building fitly framed together groweth unto a holy temple in the Lord:

In whom ye also are builded together for a habitation of God through the Spirit.

One thing have I desired of the Lord, that will I seek after: that I may dwell in the house of the Lord all the days of my life, to behold the beauty of the Lord, and to inquire in his temple.

Glorious things are spoken of thee, O city of God.

Of Zion it shall be said, This and that man was born in her: and the Highest himself shall establish her.

No weapon that is formed against thee shall prosper; and every tongue that shall rise against thee in judgment thou shalt condemn. This is the heritage of the servants of the Lord.

Additional: Psalm 46. 1–7; Psalm 84. 1–12; Psalm 122; Acts 2. 41–47.

Hymns: 6, 14, 16, 37, 70, 106, 121, 122, 127, 137, 140, 141, 144, 195, 208.

IV. The Word of God.

All Scripture is given by inspiration of God, and is profitable for doctrine, for reproof, for correction, for instruction in righteousness:

That the man of God may be perfect, thoroughly furnished unto all good works.

Search the Scriptures; for in them ye think ye have eternal life: And they are they which testify of me.

Thy counsels of old are faithfulness and truth.

Wherewith shall a young man cleanse his way? By taking heed thereto according to thy word.

Open thou mine eyes, that I may behold wondrous things out of thy law.

Thy testimonies also are my delight, and my counselors.

I will run the way of thy commandments, when thou shalt enlarge my heart.

Forever, O Lord, thy word is settled in heaven.

Thou hast magnified thy word above all thy name.

Thy testimonies have I taken as a heritage forever: for they are the rejoicing of my heart.

Depart from me, ye evildoers: for I will keep the commandments of my God.

Hold thou me up, and I shall be safe: and I will have respect unto thy statutes continually.

Thy testimonies are wonderful: therefore doth my soul keep them.

The entrance of thy words giveth light; it giveth understanding unto the simple.

Thy word is a lamp unto my feet, and a light unto my path.

I rejoice at thy word, as one that findeth great spoil.

Great peace have they which love thy law: and nothing shall offend them.

Therefore I love thy commandments above gold: yea, above fine gold.

Additional: Psalm 19. 7-11; Isa. 55. 8-11.

Hymns: 4, 12, 13, 17, 106, 108, 121, 152, 163, 209.

V. Work.

But what think ye? A certain man had two sons; and he came to the first, and said, Son, go work to-day in my vineyard.

He answered and said, I will not; but afterward he repented, and went.

And he came to the second, and said likewise. And he answered and said, I go, sir; and went not.

Whether of them twain did the will of his father? They say unto him, The first. Jesus saith unto them, Verily I say unto you, That the publicans and the harlots go into the kingdom of God before you.

As thou hast sent me into the world, even so have I also sent them into the world.

Go ye therefore, and teach all nations, baptizing them in the name of the Father, and of the Son, and of the Holy Ghost;

Teaching them to observe all things whatsoever I have commanded you: and lo, I am with you alway, even unto the end of the world.

Go ye therefore into the highways, and as many as ye shall find, bid to the marriage.

So those servants went out into the highways, and gathered together all as many as they found, both bad and good: and the wedding was furnished with guests.

Howbeit Jesus suffered him not, but saith unto him, Go home to thy friends, and tell them how great things the Lord hath done for thee, and hath had compassion on thee.

And he departed, and began to publish in Decapolis how great things Jesus had done for him: And all men did marvel.

He first findeth his own brother Simon, and saith unto him, We have found the Messias, which is, being interpreted, the Christ.

And he brought him to Jesus. And when Jesus beheld him, he said. Thou art Simon the son of Jonas: thou shalt be called Cephas, which is by interpretation, A stone.

For we are laborers together with God: ye are God's husbandry, ye are God's building.

According to the grace of God which is given unto me, as a wise master-builder, I have laid the foundation, and another buildeth thereon. But let every man take heed how he buildeth thereupon.

For other foundation can no man lay than that is laid, which is Jesus Christ.

Now if any man build upon this foundation gold, silver, precious stones, wood, hay, stubble; Every man's work shall be made manifest: for the day shall declare it, because it shall be revealed by fire; and the fire shall try every man's work of what sort it is.

If any man's work abide which he hath built thereupon, he shall receive a reward.

If any man's work shall be burned, he shall suffer loss: but he himself shall be saved; yet so as by fire.

But be ye doers of the word, and not hearers only, deceiving your own selves.

For if any be a hearer of the word, and not a doer, he is like unto a man beholding his natural face in a glass.

For he beholdeth himself, and goeth his way, and straightway forgetteth what manner of man he was.

But whoso looketh into the perfect law of liberty, and continueth therein, he being not a forgetful hearer, but a doer of the work, this man shall be blessed in his deed.

Additional: John 4. 31-38; Phil. 2. 12-16; Heb. 13. 12-16.

Hymns: 61, 66, 68, 86, 94, 101, 131, 135, 142, 149, 166.

VI. Revival Services.

1. *Exhortation.*

Seek ye the Lord while he may be found, call ye upon him while he is near.

Let the wicked forsake his way, and the unrighteous man his thoughts: and let him return unto the Lord, and he will have mercy upon him; and to our God, for he will abundantly pardon.

Wash ye, make you clean; put away the evil of your doings from before mine eyes;

Cease to do evil, learn to do well; seek judgment, relieve the oppressed, judge the fatherless, plead for the widow.

Acquaint now thyself with him, and be at peace: thereby good shall come unto thee.

Look unto me, and be ye saved, all the ends of the earth: for I am God, and there is none else.

Give glory to the Lord your God, before he cause darkness, and before your feet stumble upon the dark mountains, and, while ye look for light, he turn it into the shadow of death, and make it gross darkness.

DEVOTIONAL READINGS.

He that covereth his sins shall not prosper: but whoso confesseth and forsaketh them shall have mercy.

Hymns: 30, 33, 67, 115, 127, 166, 192.

2. Invitation.

Come unto me, all ye that labor and are heavy laden, and I will give you rest.

Take my yoke upon you, and learn of me, for I am meek and lowly in heart: and ye shall find rest unto your souls.

For my yoke is easy, and my burden is light.

And the Spirit and the bride say, Come. And let him that heareth say, Come. And let him that is athirst come. And whosoever will, let him take the water of life freely.

Come thou with us, and we will do thee good: for the Lord hath spoken good concerning Israel.

Then shall ye call upon me, and ye shall go and pray unto me, and I will hearken unto you.

And ye shall seek me, and find me, when ye shall search for me with all your heart.

Jesus said unto them, I am the bread of life: he that cometh to me shall never hunger; and he that believeth on me shall never thirst.

Hymns: 11, 28, 51, 124, 182.

3. Penitence and Confession.

Have mercy upon me, O God, according to thy loving-kindness: according unto the multitude of thy tender mercies blot out my transgressions.

Wash me thoroughly from mine iniquity, and cleanse me from my sin.

For I acknowledge my transgressions: and my sin is ever before me.

Against thee, thee only, have I sinned and done this evil in thy sight: that thou mightest be justified when thou speakest, and be clear when thou judgest.

Purge me with hyssop, and I shall be clean: wash me, and I shall be whiter than snow.

Create in me a clean heart, O God; and renew a right spirit within me.

Cast me not away from thy presence; and take not thy Holy Spirit from me.

Then will I teach transgressors thy ways; and sinners shall be converted unto thee.

The publican, standing afar off, would not lift up so much as his eyes unto heaven, but smote upon his breast, saying, God be merciful to me a sinner.

I tell you, this man went down to his house justified rather than the other: for every one that exalteth himself shall be abased; and he that humbleth himself shall be exalted.

If we confess our sins, he is faithful and just to forgive us our sins, and to cleanse us from all unrighteousness.

I acknowledged my sin unto thee, and mine iniquity have I not hid.

I said, I will confess my transgressions unto the Lord; and thou forgavest the iniquity of my sin.

Hymns: 23, 35, 43, 50, 53, 83, 125, 146, 155, 184, 187, 190, 191, 215.

4. Faith.

Sirs, what must I do to be saved?

Believe on the Lord Jesus Christ, and thou shalt be saved.

If thou shalt confess with thy mouth the Lord Jesus, and shalt believe in thine heart that God hath raised him from the dead, thou shalt be saved.

For with the heart man believeth unto righteousness; and with the mouth confession is made unto salvation.

Being justified by faith, we have peace with God through our Lord Jesus Christ.

He that believeth on him is not condemned: but he that believeth not is condemned already, because he hath not believed in the name of the only begotten Son of God.

And he said unto them, Go ye into all the world, and preach the Gospel to every creature.

He that believeth and is baptized shall be saved; but he that believeth not shall be damned.

As many as received him, to them gave he power to become the sons of God, even to them that believe on his name.

He that believeth on the Son hath everlasting life: and he that believeth not the Son shall not see life; but the wrath of God abideth on him.

Hymns: 17, 72, 118, 139, 160, 181, 201, 215, 217.

5. Rejoicing.

Whom having not seen, ye love; in whom, though now ye see him not, yet believing, ye rejoice with joy unspeakable and full of glory.

They joy before thee according to the joy in harvest, and as men rejoice when they divide the spoil.

O Lord, I will praise thee: though thou wast angry with me, thine anger is turned away, and thou comfortedst me.

The Spirit of the Lord God is upon me; because the Lord hath anointed me to preach good tidings unto the meek; he hath sent me to bind up the broken-hearted, to proclaim liberty to the captives, and the opening of the prison to them that are bound;

To proclaim the acceptable year of the Lord, and the day of vengeance of our God; to comfort all that mourn;

To appoint unto them that mourn in Zion, to give unto them beauty for ashes, the oil of joy for mourning, the garment of praise for the spirit of heaviness; that they might be called the Trees of righteousness, the planting of the Lord, that he might be glorified.

Thou hast turned for me my mourning into dancing: thou hast put off my sackcloth, and girded me with gladness.

Be glad in the Lord, and rejoice, ye righteous: shout for joy, all ye that are upright in heart.

O taste and see that the Lord is good: blessed is the man that trusteth in him.

Delight thyself also in the Lord; and he shall give thee the desires of thine heart.

Hymns: 24, 64, 134, 153, 154, 174, 175, 178, 189.

VII. Consecration.

I said, I will take heed to my ways, that I sin not with my tongue: I will keep my mouth with a bridle, while the wicked is before me.

But sanctify the Lord God in your hearts: and be ready always to give an answer to every man that asketh you a reason of the hope that is in you, with meekness and fear.

Elect according to the foreknowledge of God the Father, through sanctification of the Spirit, unto obedience and sprinkling of the blood of Jesus Christ.

Likewise reckon ye also yourselves to be dead indeed unto sin, but alive unto God through Jesus Christ our Lord.

Let not sin therefore reign in your mortal body, that you should obey it in the lusts thereof.

Put ye on the Lord Jesus Christ, and make not provision for the flesh, to fulfil the lusts thereof.

Put off concerning the former conversation the old man which is corrupt according to the deceitful lusts; and be renewed in the spirit of your mind:

And that ye put on the new man, which after God is created in righteousness and true holiness.

Put on therefore, as the elect of God, holy and beloved, bowels of mercies, kindness, humbleness of mind, meekness, long-suffering;

Forbearing one another, and forgiving one another, if any man have a quarrel against any: even as Christ forgave you, so also do ye.

And above all these things put on charity, which is the bond of perfectness.

And let the peace of God rule in your hearts, to the which also ye are called in one body; and be ye thankful.

Let the word of Christ dwell in you richly in all wisdom; teaching and admonishing one another in psalms and hymns and spiritual songs, singing with grace in your hearts to the Lord.

And whatsoever ye do in word or deed, do all in the name of the Lord Jesus, giving thanks to God and the Father by him.

If ye then be risen with Christ, seek those things which are above, where Christ sitteth on the right hand of God.

Set your affection on things above, not on things on the earth.

For ye are dead, and your life is hid with Christ in God.

And whatsoever ye do, do it heartily, as to the Lord, and not unto men.

Hymns: 19, 21, 27, 73, 83, 132, 148, 199.

The Apostles' Creed.

I believe in God the Father Almighty, Maker of heaven and earth: and in Jesus Christ, his only Son our Lord; who was conceived by the Holy Ghost, born of the Virgin Mary, suffered under Pontius Pilate; was crucified, dead, and buried; the third day he rose from the dead; he ascended into heaven, and sitteth on the right hand of God the Father Almighty; from thence he shall come to judge the quick and the dead.

I believe in the Holy Ghost; the Holy Catholic Church;* the communion of saints; the forgiveness of sins; the resurrection of the body, and the life everlasting. *Amen.*

* By the Holy Catholic Church is meant the Church of God in general.

HOLY, HOLY, HOLY.

(Tune: NICÆA.)

REGINALD HEBER.

JOHN BACCHUS DYKES.

1. Ho - ly, ho - ly, ho - ly, Lord God Al - might - y! Ear - ly in the
2. Ho - ly, ho - ly, ho - ly! all the saints a - dore thee, Casting down their
3. Ho - ly, ho - ly, ho - ly! tho' the darkness hide thee, Tho' the eye of
4. Ho - ly, ho - ly, ho - ly, Lord God Al - might - y! All thy works shall

morn - ing our song shall rise to thee; Ho - ly, ho - ly, ho - ly,
gold - en crowns a - round the glass - y sea; Cher - u - bim and seraphim
sin - ful man thy glo - ry may not see; On - ly thou art ho - ly!
praise thy name, in earth, and sky, and sea; Ho - ly, ho - ly, ho - ly,

mer - ci - ful and might - y, God in Three Per - sons, bless-ed Trin - i - ty!
fall - ing down be - fore thee, Which wert, and art, and ev - er - more shalt be.
there is none be - side thee, Per - fect in pow'r, in love, and pur - i - ty.
mer - ci - ful and might - y, God in Three Per - sons, blessed Trin - i - ty!

9

2   LOOK ALOFT!

FANNY J. CROSBY.

STEPHEN V. R. FORD.

1. Troub-led soul, why thus de-spond-ing? Je - sus knows and feels thy care;
2. Troub-led soul, be not dis-cour-aged, Lean on Christ and doubt no more;
3. Troub-led soul, for - get thy tri - als In the smile of Je - sus' face;

He has borne a great - er bur - den Than thy heart can ev - er bear:
To the ha - ven he is guid-ing— Yon - der lies the prom-ised shore.
Hope in God, for thou shalt praise him, And ex - alt his wondrous grace.

Tho' thy path be dark and drear-y, Tho' thy friends in - con-stant prove,
Leave to him thy ev - 'ry sor-row—He thy bur-dens will re - move,
E - ven now the storm is end-ing; Light is stream-ing from a - bove,

REFRAIN.

Look a - loft! the clouds are break-ing, There is rest in Je - sus' love.

3   JESUS IS MIGHTY TO SAVE.

L. W. S.

Lanta Wilson Smith.

1. Is there a sin that is tempt-ing you sore - ly, Fol - low - ing close - ly wher-
2. Is there bereavement, af-flic-tion, or sor - row, Shrouding your life in its
3. Your faith is tried by the sins that surround you, God is for - got - ten and
4. Great are the burdens the whole world is bearing, Sor - row, and sin, and tempt-

ev - er you go? Lur-ing your soul with a prom-ise of pleas-ure, On - ly to
pit - i-less gloom? Take it to him, who, ac-quaint-ed with sor-row, Felt ev - 'ry
e - vil a-bounds; Vain-ly you sigh for the prais-es of Si - on, Grieving while
a - tion, and care, Bring ev'ry tri - al at once to the Sav-iour, Has he not

CHORUS.

end in de-struc-tion and woe?)
woe, e-ven death and the tomb. } Take it to Je - sus, oh, take it to Je - sus,
sin's care-less rev-el-ry sounds.)
promised our bur-dens to bear?)

Je - sus is might-y, and will - ing to save;.. Sor - row and sin - ning shall

cease at his bid-ding, Je - sus is might - y, is might - y to save.

4 TRUST YE IN THE LORD FOREVER.

S. V. R. F.

STEPHEN V. R. FORD.

1. Trust ye in the Lord for - ev - er, He the Rock of A - ges is;
2. When the clouds and dark-ness gath - er, And the tem-pest's blast is heard;
3. If the path be rough and brok - en, Fear not: help is al - ways nigh;
4. Ask for grace it shall be giv - en When the woes of life increase;

God is might - y to de - liv - er, Ev - er - last - ing strength is his.
Fear no e - vil, but, the rath - er, Rest on God's un - fail - ing word.
Lo! the might - y God hath spok-en: "I will guide thee with mine eye!"
Faith shall wing thy pray'r to heav-en And the an - swer will be peace.

REFRAIN.

Trust ye in the Lord! Trust ye in the Lord! He the Rock of A - ges is;

Trust ye in the Lord! Trust ye in the Lord! Ev - er - last - ing strength is his.

12

5

ALL IN ALL TO ME.

MARK F. RAYMOND.

RALPH W. PRUYN.

1. My Lord is all in all to me, I noth - ing want be - side;
2. I flee for ref - uge to his side, What time I am a - fraid,
3. When doubt and fear my joys ef - face, I grasp the gold - en key
4. To serve him shall my pow'rs em - ploy, While life and strength are giv'n;

From sin and sor - row I am free, In Christ, the cru - ci - fied.
And in his strong pa - vil - ion hide, Se - cure and un - dis-mayed.
Of faith, and draw sup - plies of grace From his rich treas - u - ry.
I'll seek on earth no great - er joy, No high - er bliss in heav'n.

REFRAIN.

I lean on Je - sus' breast,.. And list - en to his voice;

Since I am his I dwell in bliss, And in his love re - joice.

6   ANGELS, FROM THE REALMS OF GLORY.

J. MONTGOMERY.

STEPHEN V. R. FORD.

1. An - gels from the realms of glo - ry, Wing your flight o'er all the earth;
2. Shepherds, in the field a - bid - ing, Watching o'er your flocks by night,
3. Sag - es, leave your con - tem - pla-tions, Bright-er vis-ions beam a - far;
4. Saints, be-fore the al - tar bend-ing, Watching long in hope and fear,
5. Sin - ners, wrung with true re-pent-ance, Doomed for guilt to end - less pains,

Ye who sang cre - a - tion's sto - ry, Now pro-claim Mes - si - ah's birth:
God with man is now re - sid - ing; Yon-der shines the in - fant light:
Seek the great De - sire of nations; Ye have seen his na - tal star;
Sud - den - ly the Lord, de-scend-ing, In his tem - ple shall ap - pear:
Jus - tice now re-vokes the sen-tence, Mer - cy calls you,—break your chains:

REFRAIN.

Come and wor - ship, Come and wor - ship, Worship Christ, the new - born King;

Come and wor - ship, Come and wor - ship, Worship Christ, the new-born King.

14

7 O COULD I SPEAK THE MATCHLESS WORTH.

(Tune: ARIEL.)

SAMUEL MEDLEY.   Arr. by LOWELL MASON.

1. O could I speak the match-less worth, O could I sound the glo-ries forth,
2. I'd sing the pre-cious blood he spilt, My ransom from the dreadful guilt
3. Well, the de-light-ful day will come When my dear Lord will bring me home,

Which in my Saviour shine, I'd soar and touch the heav'nly strings, And vie with Gabriel
Of sin, and wrath divine; I'd sing his glorious righteousness, In which all-perfect,
And I shall see his face; Then with my Saviour, Brother, Friend, A blest e-ter-ni-

while he sings In notes al-most di-vine, In notes al-most di-vine.
heav'n-ly dress My soul shall ev-er shine. My soul shall ev - er shine.
ty I'll spend, Tri-umph-ant in his grace. Tri-umph-ant in his grace.

8 GLORIA PATRI.

{ Glory be to the Father, and........ to the Son, And to the Ho-ly Ghost; }
{ As it was in the beginning, is now, and ev-er shall be, World without end, A - men. }

15

9

CHEER FOR THE GLEANERS.

(MAY BE SUNG AS A QUARTET AND CHORUS.)

A. C. F.

REV. A. C. FERGUSON.

1. Be not wea-ry with toil in the world's harvest-field, Tho' love's plea is re-
2. All thy pray'rs and thy deeds to the Mas-ter are dear; Yea, like treas-ure thine
3. Go and res-cue some soul from the bondage of sin, While prom-ise of

ject-ed with scorning; If with Je-sus ye watch, nor to wea-ri-ness yield,
alms he doth cher-ish; A me-mo-rial is kept thro' the a-ges to cheer
mer-cy is giv-en; There'll be an-gel-ic joy, while a star thou shalt win,

CHORUS.
Spirited.

Ye shall reap with great joy in the morning.
Thy .. heart, for love's deeds shall not per-ish. } "All hail!" Christ greets thee,
For thy crown of re-joic-ing in heav-en.

"Go forth, preach my word, I will bless ev-er-y faithful en-deav-or; Go,

glean precious souls for thy Master and Lord, And lo! I'll be with thee for-ev-er!"

16

S. V. R. F.
Smooth and flowing.

STEPHEN V. R. FORD.

1. Hap-py are we as we gath-er to-day, Joy-bells are ring-ing,
2. To-kens of love from our Fa-ther in heav'n—Mer-cies a-bound-ing
3. Leaning for safe-ty on God's might-y arm, Dai-ly he keeps us
4. Now to the Sav-iour our vows we re-new, Ev-er to serve him,

hear what they say: "Come, come a-way to this glad ju-bi-lee;
dai-ly are giv'n; Bless-ings as countless as stars of the night
free from all harm; O'er us his ban-ner is spread while we sleep;
faith-ful and true; Then, in the cho-rus of heav'n's ju-bi-lee,

CHORUS.

Come with your hearts full of mirth and glee."
Flow, full and free, from his throne of light.
An-gels from glo-ry their vig-ils keep.
Glo-ry to Je-sus our song shall be!

Songs of de-vo-tion to

Je-sus we raise, Earth shall re-sound with our an-thems of praise!

High as the heav'ns let the mel-o-dy ring, Glo-ry to Christ our King!

17

2

OUR SAVIOUR FOR YOU.

MARIAN FROELICH.

G. FROELICH.

1. O who is like Je - sus, the cru - ci - fied One, Our light and sal -
2. No joy to his chil-dren is ev - er de - nied: Who un - der the
3. The earth with its pleasures will soon pass a - way; The love of our

va - tion, our Shield and our Sun; Our ref - uge in troub - le, our
In - fin - ite shad - ow a - bide In - her - it all glad - ness, all
Sav - iour a - bid - eth for aye; In life or in death we shall

sol - ace in care, The Chief of ten thou-sand, the One ev - er fair.
rap - ture and bliss, And life in his love is per - pet - u - al peace.
ne'er be a - lone, With Je - sus pos-sess - ing our hearts as his throne.

REFRAIN.

Our Sav - iour so lov - ing, so pre - cious and true,

With ten - der en - treat - y we of - fer to you.

JOSEPHINE POLLARD.

C. C. CONVERSE. By per.

1. O, be joy - ful all ye lands! Shout a - loud for joy! Take your harps with-
2. Know ye that the Lord is God! Praise his ho - ly name! Know ye that the
3. En - ter in his gates with thanks! And his courts with praise! En - ter in his
4. O! how gra - cious is the Lord, Ev - er good and kind! Sing his praise with

in your hands, Shout a - loud for joy! Seek the Lord with love and joy!
Lord is God! Praise his ho - ly name! For he made us and will keep
gates with thanks! And his courts with praise! Poor re - turn our hearts can give
one ac - cord! Joined in heart and mind. For his mer - cy's ev - er sure,

Let no mind of grief an-noy, And come be - fore his presence with a song.
Faith-ful watch o'er all his sheep: Dear Shepherd of the flock and fold a - bove.
For the blessings we re-ceive: O! ev - er may our voic-es sing his praise.
And his truth will still en-dure; O! shout a - loud for joy of such a God.

CHORUS.

O, be joy - ful! Shout a-loud for joy! O, be joy-ful, Shout a-loud for joy!

13   I LOVE TO TELL THE STORY.

CATHARINE HANKEY, 1867.   WILLIAM G. FISCHER.

1. I love to tell the sto-ry, Of unseen things a-bove, Of Je-sus and his
2. I love to tell the sto-ry; More won-der-ful it seems Than all the gold-en
3. I love to tell the sto-ry; 'Tis pleasant to re-peat What seems, each time I
4. I love to tell the sto-ry; For those who know it best Seem hungering and

glo-ry, Of Je-sus and his love. I love to tell the sto-ry, Be-
fan-cies Of all our gold-en dreams. I love to tell the sto-ry, It
tell it, More won-der-ful-ly sweet. I love to tell the sto-ry; For
thirsting To hear it like the rest. And when, in scenes of glo-ry, I

cause I know it's true; It sat-is-fies my long-ings, As noth-ing else can do.
did so much for me; And that is just the reas-on I tell it now to thee.
some have never heard The message of sal-va-tion From God's own holy word.
sing the new, new song, 'Twill be the old, old sto-ry That I have loved so long.

Chorus.

I love to tell the sto-ry, 'Twill be my theme in glo-ry

To tell the old, old sto-ry Of Je-sus and his love.

CHILDREN OF ZION.

DAVID KEPPEL. STEPHEN V. R. FORD.

1. Children of Zi - on, welcome your King, Loudest ho-san - nas joy-ful-ly sing;
2. Children of Zi - on, Je - sus no more Walks as of old by Gal-i-lee's shore;
3. Children of Zi - on, loy - al and true, Do with your might what Jesus would do;
4. Children of Zi - on, joy -ful-ly sing, Je - sus is com-ing, Je - sus your King;

En - e-mies 'round him scorn and defame, Children of Zi - on, hon-or his name.
Still he can hear your songs from a-bove, Children of Zi - on, give him your love.
Je-sus, your life, your truth and your way, Children of Zi - on, trust and o - bey.
Coming to bear his ransomed ones home, Children of Zi - on, soon he will come.

REFRAIN.

Welcome your King,........ welcome your King;........ Chil-dren of

Welcome your King, wel-come your King;

Zi - on, wel-come your King; Wel-come your King,........

Wel - come your King.

wel-come your King;........ Children of Zi - on, welcome your King.

wel - come your King;

FULL SALVATION.

MARY J. ALLERTON.   EZRA D. YOUNG.

1. I am trust-ing in the Lord for full sal-va-tion, Glo-ry to his
2. He will keep me in the time of fi-'ry tri-al, Glo-ry to his
3. I am build-ing on the on-ly sure founda-tion, Glo-ry to his
4. I've a Sav-iour who is might-y to de-liv-er, Glo-ry to his

ho-ly name! He has made me free from sin and con-dem-na-tion,
ho-ly name! He has prom-ised to re-ward my self-de-ni-al,
ho-ly name! I'll a-bide the day of wrath and trib-u-la-tion,
ho-ly name! He will pi-lot me a-cross the si-lent riv-er,

REFRAIN.

Glo-ry to his ho-ly name!
Glo-ry to his ho-ly name!
Glo-ry to his ho-ly name!   Hal-le-lu-jah! Hal-le-
Glo-ry to his ho-ly name!

lu-jah! There's re-demp-tion in the Lamb for sin-ners slain: Hal-le

lu-jah! Hal-le-lu-jah! Hal-le-lu-jah! un-to him who lives a-gain!

DR. H. G. JACKSON.   JOHN B. SHAW.

1. We're march-ing to Ca-naan, the land of the blest, Where troubles all
2. The ar-mies of Sa-tan, in bat-tle ar-ray, Op-pose our ad-
3. The Jor-dan's be-fore us, a dark swell-ing tide, But Je-sus, our

cease, and the wea-ry find rest; With fields ev-er green, and with skies ev-er fair—
vance, and would turn us away; But Je-sus, our Cap-tain, is val-iant and strong,
Cap-tain, its waves will di-vide; Then cross-ing in tri-umph to yon bliss-ful shore,

CHORUS.

The home of the soul—O we soon will be there!
And, rout-ed the foe, we go march-ing a-long. } Marching to Ca-naan, we're
We'll join the dear comrades who've march'd on before.

march-ing a-long, Un-der his banner we are marching a-long; The Saviour's our

Cap-tain, Sal-va-tion our song; To Canaan, bright Canaan, we are marching along.

17 I AM WALKING BY FAITH.

(MAY BE SUNG AS A QUARTET AND CHORUS.)

S. V. R. F.

STEPHEN V. R. FORD.

1. I am walk-ing by faith in my Sav-iour and Lord, Con-tent with the
2. "I am with you al-way," lo! the voice of the Lord Rings out with this
3. If it shall be the will of my Fa-ther in heav'n To lead me through
4. And when faith at the last shall re-solve in-to sight, And Je-sus in

gifts of his love; And I know that the light from the
mes-sage of cheer; Far a-bove the wild blast of the
sor-row and care To the man-sions of rest, grace di-
glo-ry I see, I shall know that his plan for my

lamp of his word Will guide me to glo-ry a-bove:
tem-pest 'tis heard—The prom-ise that calms all my fear.
vine will be giv'n, To save me from doubt and de-spair.
guid-ance was right, And praise him whose grace res-cued me.

CHORUS.

With his right hand he hold-eth me, And so, whate'er the path may be,

I'll fear no ill, for I shall stand On Zi-on's hill, and, by his hand,

Be crowned with im - mor - tal - i - ty, Be crowned with im-mor- tal - i - ty.

18 HALLELUJAH!

ANON.

E. S. LORENZ.

1. Hal - le - lu - jah! song of glad-ness, Song of ev - er - last - ing joy; Hal - le -
2. Hal - le - lu - jah! Church victorious, Thou may'st lift this joy - ful strain; Hal - le -

CHORUS.

lu - jah! song the sweetest That can an-gels' hosts em-ploy. } Praise ye the Lord! sing
lu - jah! songs of triumph Well be - fit the ransomed train. }

1. "Near - er the cross!" my heart can say, I am com - ing near-er; Near - er the
2. Near - er the Christian's mer - cy-seat, I am com - ing near-er; Feasting my
3. Near - er in pray'r my hope as - pires, I am com - ing near-er; Deep - er the

cross from day to day, I am com - ing near-er; Near - er the cross where
soul on man - na sweet I am com - ing near-er; Stron - ger in faith, more
love my soul de-sires I am com - ing near-er; Near - er the end of

Je - sus died, Near - er the fountain's crim-son tide, Near - er my Sav-iour's
clear I see Je - sus who gave him-self for me; Near - er to him I
toil and care, Near - er the joy I long to share, Near - er the crown I

wound-ed side, I am com - ing near - er, I am com - ing near - er.
still would be; Still I'm com - ing near - er, Still I'm com-ing near - er.
soon shall wear: I am com - ing near - er, I am com - ing near - er.

26

20   THE PILGRIMS' SONG.

S. V. R. F.

STEPHEN V. R. FORD.

1. We are pil-grims on the earth, Journeying on-ward from our birth, Toward a
2. Oft we lift our long-ing eyes To the cit-y in the skies, Dear Je-
3. Soon our pil-grim-age will cease, All our tri-als end in peace, God shall

cit-y out of sight, while here we roam; O-ver Jor-dan's gold-en
ru-sa-lem the gold-en, built a-bove; Where the lov-ing Fa-ther
wipe the tears of sor-row all a-way; Songs of ev-er-last-ing

strand, Our be-lov-ed Fa-ther-land Bids us wel-come to e-ter-nal rest and home.
waits To un-fold the pearl-y gates, And re-ceive the chil-dren ran-somed by his love.
joy Shall our rap-tur'd tongues employ, Thro' the count-less a-ges of e-ter-nal day.

REFRAIN.

When the beau-ty of the morn-ing, bright and fair, Breaks up-on the crys-tal

bright and fair,

riv-er o-ver there, We shall anch-or in the har-bor, We shall

o-ver there,

gath-er on the shore, In the beau-ty of the morn-ing bright and fair bright and fair.

27

MY JESUS, AS THOU WILT.

Benjamin Schmolke.
Tr. by Miss J. Borthwick.
(Tune: Jewett.)
Carl Maria Von Weber.

1. My Je - sus, as thou wilt: O may thy will be mine;
2. My Je - sus, as thou wilt: Though seen thro' many a tear,
3. My Je - sus, as thou wilt: All shall be well for me;

In - to thy hand of love I would my all re - sign.
Let not my star of hope Grow dim or dis - ap - pear.
Each chang - ing fu - ture scene I glad - ly trust with thee.

Through sor - row or through joy, Con - duct me as thine own,
Since thou on earth hast wept And sor - rowed oft a - lone,
Straight to my home a - bove, I trav - el calm - ly on,

And help me still to say, "My Lord, thy will be done."
If I must weep with thee, "My Lord, thy will be done."
And sing in life or death, "My Lord, thy will be done."

REV. J. E. RANKIN, D.D.   EZRA D. YOUNG.

1. Watchman, is the night a - bat - ing? Sin's dark shad - ows, do they fly?
2. Lo! we see up - on the mountains Lift - ing are the mists of night;
3. God thou art, of truth and glo - ry! Hes - i - ta - ting shall we stand,
4. Still, from land to land ad - vanc - ing, Trop - ic vales, to hills of snow,

Ah! im - pa - tient souls are wait - ing, For the day-spring from on high;
Glow the gla - ciers— i - cy fountains—Touched with gleams of ear - ly light.
As we read the won - drous sto - ry Com - ing from each dis - tant land?
Light up - on their stand - ards glanc - ing, For - ward let thy le - gions go!

For the blos - som of the morn - ing, When the gloom shall flee a - way,
Many a hea - then soul is wak - ing, Bowed be - neath sin's heav - y load,
Gates of brass how thou hast brok - en, Bat - tered prej - u - di - ces down,
Send thy her - alds out be - fore thee, Back sin's heav - y por - tals swing,

And the sun, the East a - dorn - ing; Shall bring in the per - fect day.
False de - pend - en - cies for - sak - ing, Feel - ing blind - ly aft - er God.
To man's blund'ring wis - dom spok - en, From his pride stripped off the crown?
Teach the na - tions to a - dore thee, Rise and hail thee as their King.

STEPHEN V. R. FORD.

1. Sav - iour, when with sin op-pressed, To the cross I flee;
2. When temp - ta - tion's darts as - sail, Let me hide in thee;
3. When the waves of sor - row roll, Calm the troubled sea:
4. When to Jor - dan's brink I come, Let me find in thee.

Seek - ing par - don, peace and rest— In - ter - cede for me.
In thy strength I shall pre - vail - In - ter - cede for me.
Whis - per com - fort to my soul— In - ter - cede for me.
Fa - ther, wel - come, rest and home— In - ter - cede for me.

REFRAIN.

In - ter - cede for me,...... In - ter - cede for me;...... Hear my

for me. for me;

pray'r, O Lamb of God, List - en to my plea; In - ter - cede for me;.....

for me,

30

INTERCEDE FOR ME.—*Continued.*

In - ter-cede for me;..... Let thine all-a-ton-ing blood Cleanse and make me free.

for me;

---

24 SWEET LIBERTY.

S. V. R. F.

STEPHEN V. R. FORD.

1. The Son has made me free, From sor - row sin and shame; He
2. The serv - ant of the Lord I am, nor bond - age feel; His
3. He bids my doubts de - part, My griefs and fears sub - side; His
4. Christ is my lib - er - ty; My boast be on - ly this, And

REFRAIN.

gives me lib - er - ty, All glo - ry to his name!
smile is my re - ward, My joy the Spir - it's seal.
tem - ple is my heart, While I in him a - bide.
in e - ter - ni - ty, The glo - ry shall be his.

Sweet lib - er - ty

Sweet lib - er - ty, In Christ I have sweet lib - er - ty.

31

25 WONDROUS LOVE.

MAGGIE E. GREGORY.

S. F. ACKLEY.

1. Oh my Sav - iour, how I love thee, Thou did'st shed thy blood for me,
2. Blessed Je - sus, how I love thee, Mind, and strength, and heart, and soul,
3. Oh my Sav - iour, how I love thee, Nev - er was a love like thine;
4. Oh my Sav - iour, how I love thee, For sal - va - tion full and free;
5. Oh my Sav - iour, how I love thee, Thou dost smile from heaven above,
6. Blessed Sav - iour, how I love thee, How I bless thee and a - dore,

Thou did'st give thy life to save me, Naught will I with-hold from thee.
Help me tell the wondrous sto - ry, How thy pow'r hath made me whole.
Thou hast purchased my re-demption, I am saved by love di - vine.
All my life shall be de - vot - ed Un - to him who died for me.
Thou dost guide me by thy Spir - it, Thou dost fill with per - fect love.
Source of life, and light, and lov-ing, Teach me, Lord, to love thee more.

CHORUS.

Wondrous love that seal'd my par-don, Wondrous love that makes me free;

Wondrous love that died for sin - ners, Teach me, Lord, to love like thee.

WHAT A FRIEND WE HAVE IN JESUS.

JOSEPH SCRIVEN.

CHARLES C. CONVERSE. By per.

1. What a friend we have in   Je - sus,   All   our sins and griefs to bear!
2. Have we tri - als and tempt - a - tions? Is there troub-le a - ny - where?
3. Are we weak and heav - y - la - den, Cumbered with a load of care?—

What a priv-i-lege to car - ry Ev - ery thing to God in prayer!
We should nev-er be dis - cour - aged, Take it to the Lord in prayer.
Pre - cious Saviour, still our ref - uge,— Take it to the Lord in prayer.

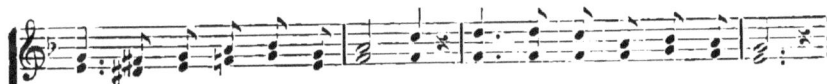

O what peace we oft - en for - feit, O what need-less pain we bear,
Can we find a friend so faith - ful Who will all our sor-rows share?
Do thy friends de-spise, for-sake thee? Take it to the Lord in prayer;

All be - cause we do not car - ry Ev - ery thing to God in prayer!
Je - sus knows our ev - ery weak-ness, Take it to the Lord in prayer.
In his arms he'll take and shield thee, Thou wilt find a sol - ace there.

CLEANSING WAVE.

PHŒBE PALMER.

MRS. JOSEPH F. KNAPP.

1. O, now I see the crim-son wave, The fount-ain deep and wide, Je-
2. I rise to walk in heaven's own light, A-bove the world and sin, With
3. A-maz-ing grace! 'tis heaven be-low, To feel the blood ap-plied, And

sus, my Lord, might-y to save, Points to his wound-ed side.
heart made pure, and garments white, And Christ en-throned with-in.
Je-sus, on-ly Je-sus know, My Je-sus cru-ci-fied.

REFRAIN.

The cleansing stream, I see, I see! I plunge, and O, it cleanseth me! O,

praise the Lord, it cleans-eth me! It cleans-eth me, yes, cleans-eth me!

28   COME, SINNERS, TO THE GOSPEL FEAST.

C. Wesley.   Ezra D. Young.

1. Come, sin - ners, to   the   gos - pel feast, Let   ev - 'ry soul   be
2. Sent   by my Lord,   on   you   I   call; The   in - vi - ta - tion
3. Come, all ye souls by   sin   oppressed, Ye   rest - less wan-d'rers
4. My mes - sage as   from God re - ceive; Ye   all may come to
5. See him set forth be - fore your eyes, That pre - cious, bleed-ing

Je - sus' guest; Ye need not one   be   left be - hind, For
is   to   all: Come all   the world! come, sin - ner, thou! All
aft - er rest; Ye   poor, and maimed, and halt, and blind, In
Christ and live: O   let   his love your hearts con - strain, Nor
sac - ri - fice: His of - fered ben - e - fits em - brace, And

REFRAIN.

God hath bid - den all mankind.
things in Christ are read - y now.
Christ a heart - y welcome find.   } Come, while the gos - pel feast is spread, And
suf - fer him to   die in vain.
free - ly now be saved by grace.

feed on Christ the liv - ing bread, And feed on Christ the liv - ing bread.

Copyright, 1894, by Hunt & Eaton, New York.

ANGELS, ROLL THE ROCK AWAY.

THOMAS SCOTT.

STEPHEN V. R. FORD.

1. An - gels, roll the rock a - way! Death, yield up the might - y Prey!
2. Shout, ye ser - aphs; an - gels, raise Your e - ter - nal song of praise;
3. Ho - ly Fa - ther, Ho - ly Son, Ho - ly Spir - it, Three in One,

See, the Sav - iour quits the tomb, Glow - ing with im - mor - tal bloom.
Let the earth's re - mot - est bound Ech - o to the bliss - ful sound.
Glo - ry as of old to thee, Now and ev - er - more shall be.

REFRAIN.

Al - le - lu - ia! Al - le - lu - ia! Christ the Lord is ris'n to - day;

Al - le - lu - ia! Al - le - lu - ia! Christ the Lord is ris'n to - day.

THE PEARLY GATES ARE OPEN.

"The gates of it shall not be shut."—Rev. xxi, 25.

MARK F. RAYMOND.　　　　　　　　　　　　　　　EZRA D. YOUNG.

1. O have you heard the news To wea - ry mor - tals giv'n,
2. Ye bells of heav'n and earth Ring out the gold - en psalm!
3. No pil - grim saved from sin, Thro' Christ's a - ton - ing blood,
4. How blest are they whose names Are writ in heav'n a - bove!
5. Ho! wea - ry, home-less souls, From sin and death a - rise!

To cheer them in their pil - grim-age A - long the way to heav'n?
Pro-claim the news in joy - ful strains, Ye followers of the Lamb.
E'er sought in vain to en - ter in The cit - y of our God.
Who jour - ney on in pa - tient faith, Sustained by hope and love.
Re - pent, be - lieve, and win, thro' Christ, A man - sion in the skies.

REFRAIN.

The pearl - - - y gates of Par - - - - a - dise

The pearl - y gates of Par - a - dise, The pearl - y gates of Par - a - dise

Are o - pen wide to - day, Are o - pen wide to - day!

REVIVE US AGAIN.

WM. PATON MACKAY.

J. J. HUSBAND.

1. We praise thee, O God! for the Son of thy love, For Je - sus who
2. We praise thee, O God! for thy spir - it of light, Who has shown us our
3. All glo - ry and praise to the Lamb that was slain, Who has borne all our
4. All glo - ry and praise to the God of all grace, Who has bought us, and
5. Re - vive us a - gain; fill each heart with thy love; May each soul be re -

CHORUS.

died, and is now gone a - bove. }
Sav - iour and scattered our night. }
sins, and has cleansed every stain. } Hal - le - lu - jah! thine the glo - ry; Hal - le -
sought us, and guid - ed our ways. }
kin - dled with fire from a - bove. }

lu - jah! A - men! Hal - le - lu - jah! thine the glo - ry; Re - vive us a - gain.

32   REJOICE AND BE GLAD.

1 Rejoice and be glad! the Redeemer has come!
  Go look on his cradle, his cross, and his tomb.

CHORUS.—Sound his praises, tell the story of him who was slain;
  Sound his praises, tell with gladness, he liveth again.

2 Rejoice and be glad! it is sunshine at last!
  The clouds have departed, the shadows are past.—*Cho.*

3 Rejoice and be glad! for the blood hath been shed;
  Redemption is finished, the price hath been paid.—*Cho.*

4 Rejoice and be glad! now the pardon is free!
  The Just for the unjust has died on the tree.—*Cho.*

5 Rejoice and be glad! for the Lamb that was slain
  O'er death is triumphant, and liveth again.—*Cho.*

6 Rejoice and be glad! for our King is on high,
  He pleadeth for us on his throne in the sky. —*Cho.*

7 Rejoice and be glad! for he cometh again;
  He cometh in glory, the Lamb that was slain. *Cho.*

REV. HORATIUS BONAR. 1874.

MARY J. ALLERTON.　　　　　　　　　　　ROBERT PAYSON.

1. Christ is call - ing thee to - day, Heark - en, sin - ner, to his voice;
2. Sin and death pur - sue thy soul; To the cross for ref - uge flee;
3. Christ en-treats thee: why de - lay? Hast - en, ere it be too late:
4. Now the lov - ing Sav - iour pleads: Choose the way in which he trod;

Heed the sum - mons and o - bey, Make the Lord of hosts your choice.
Christ can make the wounded whole, He hath purchased life for thee.
Death may sum - mon thee a - way And for - ev - er seal thy fate.
Fol - low him whose path - way leads To the cit - y of our God.

REFRAIN.

Fol - low me, come, fol - low me; Leave the world and sin be - hind;

Life and im - mor - tal - i - ty In my serv - ice thou shalt find.

34 MY REDEEMER.

MARIAN FROELICH.

G. FROELICH.

1. My heart is filled with pur-est love, For Christ, my soul's sal-va-tion;
2. Had gold or sil-ver been the price, Of free-dom from op-pres-sion,
3. On earth my heav-en is be-gun, Since Christ my soul pos-sess-es,

My spir-it mounts to heav'n a-bove, On wings, of ad-o-ra-tion.
The mines of earth would not suf-fice To pur-chase its pos-ses-sion.
And in my skies there beams a sun That ev-ery mo-ment bless-es;

I hon-or him who sought me out, Who res-cued me from
Un-done I felt my lost es-tate, And trem-bling knocked at
O bound-less love! I mer-it naught, But Je-sus hath my

REFRAIN.

Christ, my soul's Re - deem - er.)
sus, my soul's Re - deem - er. }
Christ, mysoul's Re - deem - er.)

My.... Re - deem - er, my.... Re -
My Re - deem - er, my Re -

deem - er, Sal - va - tion full in me he wrought, Bless him my soul's Re-deem-er.

35   JESUS! HEAR MY PRAYER.

(Tune: MEDIATION.)

S. V. R. F.   STEPHEN V. R. FORD.

1. Sav - iour, to thy cross I fly; Par-d'ning mer - cy is my cry;
2. Wea - ry, faint and sore dis-tressed, Full of sin, with guilt op-pressed,
3. In - ter - cede for me, O Lord; Turn a - side th'a - veng-ing sword;
4. Thou a - lone my ref - uge art, Thou canst cleanse my sin - ful heart,
5. Ho - ly Spir - it, light di - vine, In my dark - ened na - ture shine;

Save me quick - ly or I die, Je - sus! hear my pray'r...
To thine arms I flee for rest, Je - sus! hear my pray'r...
Speak the rec - on - cil - ing word,— Je - sus! hear my pray'r...
Par - don, peace and life im - part,— Je - sus! hear my pray'r...
Make and seal me ev - er thine, Je - sus! hear my pray'r...

THE NAME OF MY REDEEMER.

MARK F. RAYMOND.

EZRA D. YOUNG.

1. The name of my Re-deem-er Is pre-cious to my heart,
2. It brings a ho-ly com-fort To hearts with an-guish riv'n,
3. It seals with joy of par-don The sin-sick, con-trite soul,
4. O won-drous name of Je-sus! The shin-ing hosts a-bove,

It scat-ters all my sor-rows, And bids my fears de-part.
It turns their grief to glad-ness, Their sighs to songs of heav'n.
It heals the brok-en-heart-ed, And makes the wound-ed whole.
Fall down in ad-o-ra-tion Be-fore the name I love.

REFRAIN.

O bless-ed name of Je-sus! I'll sing it o'er and o'er;

For ev-'ry time I sing it, I love it more and more.

SABINE BARING-GOULD. ARTHUR SEYMOUR SULLIVAN.

1. Onward, Christian soldiers! Marching as to war, With the cross of Je - sus
2. At the sign of tri-umph Satan's host doth flee; On, then, Christian soldiers,
3. Like a might-y arm-y Moves the Church of God; Brothers, we are tread-ing
4. Crowns and thrones may perish, Kingdoms rise and wane, But the Church of Jesus
5. Onward, then, ye peo-ple! Join our happy throng, Blend with ours your voices

Go-ing on be-fore. Christ, the roy-al Mas - ter, Leads a-gainst the foe;
On to vic-to-ry! Hell's founda-tions quiv - er At the shout of praise;
Where the saints have trod; We are not di - vid - ed, All one bod - y we,
Constant will remain; Gates of hell can nev - er 'Gainst that Church prevail;
In the triumph-song; Glo - ry, laud, and hon - or Un - to Christ the King,

CHORUS.

Forward in-to bat - tle, See, his banners go! ⎞
Brothers, lift your voi-ces, Loud your athems raise. ⎟
One in hope and doc-trine, One in char - i - ty. ⎬ Onward, Christian sol-diers!
We have Christ's own promise, And that cannot fail. ⎟
This thro' countless a - ges Men and angels sing. ⎠

Marching as to war, With the cross of Je - sus Go-ing on be-fore.

38   IN THE DEW. (*An Epworth League Hymn.*)

Minnie W. Baines-Miller.   Stephen V. R. Ford.

1. Your sick-les swing in the dew, While the morn of life is new.
2. Wait not til the noon is high And its sunbeams tor-rid lie,
3. Wait not till the slant-ing sun Marks the short day al-most done.

And its ear-ly beams Have the hues of dreams Most beau-ti-ful to view.
With their rose-tints gone, All the parch'd lield is on, And the heat and bur-den vie.
And the ti-ed flow'rs, And the wast-ed hours, And the sheaves you have not won.

Your sick-les swing in the dew, While the morn of life is new;
Wait not till the noon is high, And its sunbeams tor-rid lie;
Wait not till the slant-ing sun Marks the short day al-most done;

Your sick-les swing in the dew, While the morn of life is new.
Wait not till the noon is high, And its sunbeams tor-rid lie.
Wait not till the slant-ing sun Marks the short day al-most done.

44

39 THE TEMPERANCE CRUSADE.

(Air: "The Battle Hymn of the Republic.")

Rev. D. Williams.

1. The light of truth is breaking, on the mountain tops it gleams; Let it
2. With purpose strong and steady, in the great Jehovah's name, We will
3. Our strength is in Jehovah, and our cause is in his care; With Al-

flash a-long our valleys, let it glitter on our streams, Till
rise to snatch our kindred from the depths of woe and shame, And the
mighty arms to help us, we have faith to do and dare, While con-

all our land a-wak-ens in its flush of gold-en beams; Our
ju-bi-lee of free-dom to the slaves of sin pro-claim; Our
fid-ing in the prom-ise that the Lord will an-swer pray'r: Our

CHORUS.

God is marching on.
God is marching on. Glo-ry, glo-ry hal-le-lu-jah! Glo-ry, glo-ry hal-le-
God is marching on.

lu-jah! Glo-ry, glo-ry hal-le-lu-jah! Our God is march-ing on.

49

40

O, TO BE THERE!

FROM THE DUTCH.　　　　　　(QUARTET.)　　　　　　STEPHEN V. R. FORD.

1. O, to be there! O, to be there! Where nev - er
2. O, love - ly home! O, love - ly home! Thy fra - grant,
3. O, let me go! O, let me go! Death shall not
4. For thou art there! For thou art there! Who un - to

tears of sor - row Shall dim the eye, nor ach - ing
thorn - less flow - ers Droop not nor die, but ev - er -
there dis - sev - er Our lov - ing hearts, where streams of
me hath giv - en E - ter - nal life, and made me

pain nor care Shall o - - - ver - - cloud the
last - ing bloom Crowns all........ thy gold - en
pleas - ure flow At God's........ right hand for -
pure and fair, And this........ to me is

mor - row; O, to be there! O, to be there!
hours; O, to be there! O, to be there!
ev - er; O, let me go! O, let me go!
heav - en; For thou art there! For thou art there!

WE BRING NO GLITTERING TREASURES.

HARRIET PHILLIPS.

Arr. from SILCHER.

1. We bring no glit-t'ring treas-ures, No gems from earth's deep mine;
2. The dear - est gift of heav - en, Love's writ-ten word of truth,
3. Re - deem - er, grant thy bless - ing! O teach us how to pray,

We come, with sim - ple meas - ures, To chant thy love di - vine.
To us is ear - ly giv - en, To guide our steps in youth;
That each, thy fear pos - sess - ing, May tread life's on - ward way.

Chil - dren, thy fav - ors shar - ing, Their voice of thanks would raise;......
We hear the wondrous sto - ry, The tale of Cal - va - ry;........
Then, where the pure are dwell-ing, We hope to meet a - gain,......

Fa - ther, ac - cept our of - f'ring, Our song of grate - ful praise.
We read of homes in glo - ry, From sin and sor - row free.
And, sweet - er num - bers swell - ing, For - ev - er praise thy name.

42   IN JESUS' LOVE ABIDING.

S. V. R. F.

STEPHEN V. R. FORD.

1. In   Je - sus' love a - bid - ing,   And with his pres-ence blest,
2. In   times of   trib - u - la - tion,   When hope grows faint and dim,
3. He   car - ries all my   sor - rows,   And makes my bur - dens his;
4. And   so   in him a - bid - ing,   My   earth - ly race I'll run

He   fills my soul with   rapt - ure,   And gives me sweet - est   rest.
He   calms my troub - led   spir - it,   Be - cause I   trust in   him.
He   temp - ers my   af - flic - tions,   And fills my   soul with   bliss.
With pa - tience, till in   glo - ry   The crown of   life   is   won.

REFRAIN.

There is rest,   sweet rest,   In Je - sus' love a - bid - ing,
There is rest,   sweet rest,

And   in   his   word con - fid - ing, There is   rest, sweet rest.

Copyright, 1894, by Hunt & Eaton, New York.

43   CAST THY BURDEN ON THE LORD.

S. V. R. F.

STEPHEN V. R. FORD.

Moderato. DUET, SOP. & ALTO.   QUARTET.

1. Is thy soul with sin oppressed? Cast thy bur - den on the Lord;
2. Is thy heart o'erwhelmed with grief? Cast thy bur - den on the Lord;
3. Dost thou dread the si - lent tomb? Cast thy bur - den on the Lord;
4. Would'st thou reign with Christ above?Cast thy bur - den on the Lord;

DUET, SOP. & ALTO.   QUARTET.

He will sure - ly give thee rest, Cast thy bur - den on the Lord.
He will give thee sweet re - lief, Cast thy bur - den on the Lord.
He hath scattered all its gloom, Cast thy bur - den on the Lord.
Trust in his re - deem-ing love, Cast thy bur - den on the Lord.

CHORUS.

All thy sins to Je - sus bring - ing, All thy sor - row guilt and woe;

To the cross of Je - sus cling - ing, He will wash thee white as snow......
white as snow.

4   49

WORTHY THE LAMB.

REV. H. L. HASTINGS.

REV. SAMUEL ALMAN. By per.

1. Hark! from the mansions of glo - ry the song, "Worthy the Lamb that was slain!"
2. We here on earth would assist in the strain, Worthy the Lamb that was slain:
3. Soon shall we shout by the side of the King, Worthy the Lamb that was slain:

Thousands of an - gels the an - them prolong, Worthy the Lamb that was slain.
We would take up the glad an - them a-gain, Worthy the Lamb that was slain.
Soon with the an - gels his praise we shall sing, Worthy the Lamb that was slain.

Loud as the thunder's re-ech-o - ing roar, Loud as the billows that dash on the shore,
He hath redeem'd us from sin and from woe, Taught us his mercy and glo - ry to know,
Soon in his glory and pow'r he shall come, Soon shall he gather his ransomed ones home,

Sweet on the notes which the glad harpers pour, Worthy the Lamb that was slain.
Ev - er his rap-tur-ous praise we would show, Worthy the Lamb that was slain.
Then shall we shout as we sit on his throne, Worthy the Lamb that was slain.

H. P. DANKS.

Moderato.

1. I am wea - ry of stray - ing; Oh! fain would I rest
2. I am wea - ry of hop - ing, where hope is un - true,
3. I am wea - ry of sigh - ing; o'er sor - rows of earth,
4. I am wea - ry of lov - ing; what pass - es a - way;
5. I am wea - ry, my Sav - iour, of griev - ing thy love;

In the far dis - tant land of the pure and the blest,
As　　　　 fair, but as fleet - ing, as morn - ing's bright dew:
O'er　　 joy's glow - ing vis - ions, that fade at their birth;
The　　 sweet - est, the dear - est, a - las! may not stay;
Oh!　　 when shall I rest in thy pres - ence a - bove?

Where　 sin can no lon - ger its bland - ish - ments spread,
I　　　　 long for the land, whose blest prom - ise a - lone
O'er the pangs of the loved, which we can - not as - suage;
I　　　　 long for the land where these part - ings are o'er,
I　　　　 am wea - ry, but oh! let me nev - er repine,

And　 tears and tempt - a - tions for - ev - er have fled.
Is　　 change - less, and sure as E - ter - ni - ty's throne.
O'er the blight - ings of youth, and the weak - ness of age.
And　 death and the tomb can di - vide hearts no more.
While thy word, and thy love, and thy prom - ise are mine.

Copyright, 1894, by H. P. Danks.

WESLEY P. MORSE. REV. W. G. COOPER.

1. When I hear the voice of an - gels, Call-ing me in tones of love,
2. I have read of that glad re - gion, That blest land of pure de - light,
3. In that bless-ed land of prom-ise, That blest land so bright and fair,

From this world of pain and sor - row To that brighter land a - bove;
Where the saints are ev - er hap - py, And ap-pear in robes of white;
I shall meet with friends and kindred—We shall know each oth - er there;

When I en - ter death's dark val - ley, Bid all earth - ly friends a - dieu;
Where the streets are bright and glis - ten, In the Lamb's re-splendent glow;
And with them shall dwell for - ev - er, Free from care, grief, pain and woe;

I will place my trust in Je - sus, He will lead me safe - ly thro'.
And the tree of life is bloom - ing, Where the liv - ing wa - ters flow.
Naught but joy can ev - er en - ter, Where the liv - ing wa - ters flow.

CHORUS.

This life will soon be end - ed, My days are few, I know,

52

But I hope to gain the ha-ven, Where the liv-ing wa-ters flow.

47   ALL TO CHRIST I OWE.

MRS. E. M. HALL.   JOHN T. GRAPE.

1. I hear the Sav-iour say, Thy strength in-deed is small; Child of
2. Lord, now in-deed I find Thy faith, and thine a-lone, Can
3. For noth-ing good have I Where-by thy grace to claim— I'll
4. When from my dy-ing bed My ran-somed soul shall rise, Then
5. And when be-fore the throne I stand in him com-plete, I'll

CHORUS.

weakness, watch and pray, Find in me thine all in all.
change the lep-er's spots, And melt the heart of stone.
wash my garment white In the blood of Calv'ry's Lamb.   Je-sus paid it all,
"Je-sus paid it all" Shall rend the vault-ed skies.
lay my tro-phies down, All down at Je-sus' feet.

All to him I owe; Sin had left a crimson stain; He washed it white as snow.

53

MARY J. ALLERTON.   ROBERT PAYSON.

1. There's a song the ran-somed sing, Round the throne of God in glo - ry,
2. These are God's e - lect who came, Out of ev - 'ry tribe and na - tion,
3. If we learn re-demp-tion's song, Ere we cross the si - lent riv - er,
4. When the storms of life are past, With the ransomed gone be - fore us,

In the presence of their King They re - peat the grand old sto - ry.
Saved by faith in Je - sus' name, Pu - ri - fied thro' trib - u - la - tion.
We shall join the white-robed throng, Sing-ing praise to Christ for - ev - er.
We shall all u - nite at last In the grand tri - umph-al cho - rus.

REFRAIN.

Un - to him who hath redeemed us, And washed us in his precious blood;

Glo - ry, hon - or, power and bless - ing Be to Christ the Lamb of God.

F. W. Faber.   John Bacchus Dykes.

1. Hark, hark, my soul! an-gel-ic songs are swelling O'er earth's green fields and
2. On-ward we go, for still we hear them singing, "Come, wea-ry souls, for
3. Far, far a-way, like bells at eve-ning peal-ing, The voice of Je-sus
4. Rest comes at length tho' life be long and drear-y; The day must dawn, and
5. An-gels, sing on! your faith-ful watch-es keeping; Sing us sweet fragments

o-cean's wave-beat shore; How sweet the truth those blessed strains are tell-ing
Je-sus bids you come;" And thro' the dark, its ech-oes sweet-ly ring-ing,
sounds o'er land and sea, And la-den souls by thousands, meek-ly steal-ing,
darksome night be past; All journeys end in wel-come to the wea-ry,
of the songs a-bove; Till morning's joy shall end the night of weep-ing,

CHORUS.

Of that new life when sin shall be no more!
The mu-sic of the gos-pel leads us home.
Kind Shepherd, turn their wea-ry steps to thee. } An-gels of Je-sus,
And heav'n, the heart's true home, will come at last.
And life's long shad-ows break in cloud-less sky.

an-gels of light, Sing-ing to wel-come the pil-grims of the night!

Sing-ing to wel-come the pil-grims, the pil-grims of the night!

NOT WORTHY.

Sir H. W. Baker.

C. C. Converse. By per.

1. I am not wor - thy, Ho - ly Lord, That thou shouldst come to me; Speak
2. I am not wor - thy; cold and bare The lodg - ing of my soul; How
3. I am not wor - thy, yet, my God, How can I say thee nay; Thee
4. O come! in this sweet sa - cred hour; Feed me with food di - vine, And

but the word; one gra - cious word Can set the sin - ner free.
canst thou deign to en - ter there? Lord, speak, and make me whole.
who didst give thy flesh and blood My ran - som - price to pay?
fill with all thy love and pow'r This worth - less heart of mine.

Chorus.

Not wor - thy, not wor - thy that Thou shouldst come to me; Speak

but the word, one gra - cious word, And set the sin - ner free.

Copyright, 1-92, by C. C. Converse.

51   HO! EVERY ONE THAT THIRSTS.

JOHN WESLEY.   EZRA D. YOUNG.

1. Ho!   ev - ery one that thirsts, draw nigh, 'Tis God in - vites the fall - en race;
2. Come to   the liv - ing   wa - ters, come! Sinners, o - bey your Mak - er's call;
3. See from   the Rock a   fountain rise; For you in heal-ing streams it rolls;
4. Noth-ing   ye in   ex-change shall give; Leave all ye have and are be - hind;

Mer - cy   and free sal - va - tion buy, Buy wine, and milk, and gos - pel grace.
Re - turn,   ye wea-ry wand'rers, home, And find his grace is free for all.
Mon - ey   ye need not bring, nor price, Ye la-b'ring, burdened, sin - sick souls.
Frank-ly   the gift of   God re-ceive; Par-don and peace in Je - sus find.

REFRAIN.

Sal - va - tion's free! Sal - vation's free! The call rings out from Cal - va - ry;

Ho!   ev-ery one that thirsts, draw nigh Mer - cy and free sal - va - tion buy.

S. V. R. F. STEPHEN V. R. FORD.

1. Home at last in the dear Fa-ther-land, When the storms of life are o'er;
2. In the place he has gone to pre-pare, We shall see our ris-en Lord;
3. In the tem-ple of God we shall meet, To go out no more for aye;
4. When our con-flicts and tri-als are past, We will lay our ar-mor down;

On the banks of the riv-er we'll stand, With the loved ones gone be-fore.
To be like him, whose im-age we bear, Shall be our di-vine re-ward.
We shall walk thro' the bright gold-en street, In the realms of end-less day.
With the ransomed we'll sing, "Home at Last," And re-ceive the fade-less crown.

CHORUS.

Home at last, Home at last, Where the wea-ry are at rest;

at last, at last, at rest;

Home at last, Home at last In the mansions of the blest, of the blest.

rit.

at last, at last blest.

58

53 WHITER THAN SNOW.

JAMES NICHOLSON.   WILLIAM G. FISCHER.

1. Lord Je - sus, I long to be per - fect-ly whole; I want thee for-ev - er, to
2. Lord Je - sus, look down from thy throne in the skies, And help me to make a com-
3. Lord Je - sus, for this I most hum-bly en - treat; I wait, bless-ed Lord, at thy
4. Lord Je - sus, thou seest I pa-tient - ly wait; Come now, and with-in me a

live in my soul; Break down ev - ery i - dol, cast out ev - ery foe; Now
plete sac-ri - fice; I give up my - self, and what-ev - er I know—Now
cru - ci - fied feet, By faith, for my cleansing, I see thy blood flow—Now
new heart cre-ate; To those who have sought thee, thou never said'st No—Now

CHORUS.

wash me, and I shall be whit - er than snow.
wash me, and I shall be whit - er than snow.
wash me, and I shall be whit - er than snow.
wash me, and I shall be whit - er than snow.

Whit - er than snow, yes,

whit - er than snow; Now wash me, and I shall be whit - er than snow.

59

BLESSED NAME.

Leah Carlton.

Rev. S. Alman.

1. Bless-ed name a-bove all oth-ers, Name that most we love to sing;
2. Bless-ed name that calms our sor-rows, Takes our ev - ery fear a - way;
3. Bless-ed name, whose lov-ing kind-ness Gilds with light the sa - cred page;

O how sweet its brightest whis-per, Name of Christ, our Sav-iour King.
Gives us, when our lives are dark-est, Glimpses of... e - ter - nal day.
Bless-ed name, the saints in glo - ry Hail with joy .. from age to age.

In that name our pray'rs we of - fer, By that name our hearts are won;
Bless-ed name, our shield and buck-ler; Bless-ed name, our bat - tle - cry;
Bless-ed name a - bove all oth - ers, Name in earth and heav'n a - dored;

Gifts we ask from God the Fa - ther, In the name of Christ, the Son.
How it arms the soul with cour-age, How it bids the tempt-er fly.
Praised, re-vered by men and an - gels, Bless-ed name of Christ our Lord.

REFRAIN.

Bless-ed name.. a-bove all oth - ers, Name that most we love to sing;
Bless-ed name, bless-ed name, Name that most we

O how sweet.. its lightest whis - per, Name of Christ our Saviour King.
O how sweet, O how sweet,

55 O SAVIOUR, PRECIOUS SAVIOUR.

FRANCES R. HAVERGAL.   H. P. DANKS.

1. O Saviour, precious Saviour, Whom yet un-seen we love; O name of might and
2. O bring-er of sal-va-tion, Who wondrously hath wrought, Thyself the rev-e-
3. In thee all fulness dwelleth, All grace and pow'r di-vine; The glo-ry that ex-

CHORUS.

fa - vor, All oth-er names a - bove.
a - tion Of love beyond our thought. } We wor-ship thee, we bless thee, To
cel - leth, O Son of God, is thine.

thee a - lone we sing; We praise thee and confess thee, Our ho-ly Lord and King!

HARK! THE THOUSAND HARPS AND VOICES.

(Tune, "HARWELL.")

THOS. KELLY.   DR. LOWELL MASON.

1. Hark! ten thousand harps and voic - es Sound the note of praise a - bove;
2. King of glo - ry! reign for ev - er—Thine an ev - er - last - ing crown;
3. Sav - iour! hast - en thine ap - pear - ing; Bring, oh, bring the glo - rious day,

Je - sus reigns, and heav'n re - joic - es; Je - sus reigns, the God of love:
Nothing, from thy love, shall sev - er Those whom thou hast made thine own;—
When, the aw - ful sum - mons hear - ing, Heav'n and earth shall pass a - way;—

See, he sits on yon-der throne; Je-sus rules the world a - lone.
Hap - py ob - jects of thy grace, Destined to be-hold thy face.
Then, with golden harps, we'll sing,— "Glo - ry, glo-ry to our King!"

See, he sits   Je - sus rules

Hal - le - lu - jah, Hal - le - lu - jah, Hal - le - lu - jah! A - men.

S. V. R. F.

S. V. R. FORD.

1. We are soldiers in the ar - my of Je - ho - vah, And we're under marching
2. Just and ho - ly is our cause, and yet the con - flict May be fierce and long, for
3. O what joy to know that in this might-y war - fare Je - sus and his trust-ed

or - ders from our King (from our King); Christ has promised in his word to go be -
might - y is the foe (is the foe); Where the Saviour leads us we will glad-ly
soldiers al - ways win (al - ways win)! O what bliss to meet a - round the throne in

REF.—March - ing,

fore us, He will lead us on to vic-t'ry while we sing:
fol - low, Trusting in the Lord Je - ho - vah as we go.   } Marching, marching
glo - ry, With the millions who have conquer'd self and sin:

march - ing.   March-ing 'neath the ban - ner of the cross;

'neath the ban-ner, Marching 'neath the banner, 'neath the ban-ner of the cross;

March - ing,   march - ing.

Marching, marching for our Captain, For our Captain counting all but loss.

JERUSALEM THE GOLDEN.

(Tune: EWING.)

BERNARD OF CLUNY.   ALEXANDER EWING.

1. Je - ru - sa - lem the gold - en, With milk and hon - ey blest,
2. They stand, those halls of Zi - on, All ju - bi - lant with song,
3. There is the throne of Da - vid; And there, from care re - leased,
4. O sweet and bless - ed count - ry, The home of God's e - lect!

Be - neath thy con - tem - pla - tion Sink heart and voice op - pressed:
And bright with many an an - gel, And all the mar - tyr throng:
The song of them that tri - umph, The shout of them that feast;
O sweet and bless - ed coun - try That ea - ger hearts ex - pect.

I know not, O I know not What so - cial joys are there;
The Prince is ev - er in them, The day - light is se - rene:
And they who, with their Lead - er, Have con - quered in the fight.
Je - sus, in mer - cy bring us To that dear land of rest;

What ra - dian - cy of glo - ry, What light be - yond com - pare.
The pas - tures of the bless - ed Are decked in glo - rious sheen.
For - ev - er and for - ev - er Are clad in robes of white.
Who art, with God the Fa - ther, And Spir - it, ev - er blest.

J. MONTGOMERY. CAREY BOGGESS.

1. Songs of praise the an - gels sang—Heav'n with hal - le - lu - jahs rang,
2. Heav'n and earth must pass a - way—Songs of praise shall crown that day;
3. Saints be - low, with heart and voice, Still in songs of praise re - joice—

When Je - ho - vah's work be - gun, When he spake, and it was done.
God will make new heav'ns, new earth— Songs of praise shall be their birth.
Learn-ing here, by faith and love, Songs of praise to sing a - bove.

Songs of praise a - woke the morn, When the Prince of Peace was born;
And shall man a - lone be dumb, Till that glo - rious king - dom come?
Borne up - on their lat - est breath Songs of praise shall con - quer death;

Songs of praise a - rose when he Cap - tive led cap - tiv - i - ty.
No; the church de - lights to raise Psalms and hymns and songs of praise.
Then, a - mid e - ter - nal joy, Songs of praise their pow'rs em - ploy.

5

Rev. W. D. Cornell, Alt.   Rev. W. G. Cooper.

1. Far a-way in the depths of my spir-it to-night, Rolls a
2. What a treas-ure I have in this won-der-ful peace, Bur-ied
3. I am rest-ing to-night in this won-der-ful peace, Rest-ing
4. And me-thinks when I rise to that Cit-y of peace, Where the
5. Ah! soul are you here with-out com-fort or rest, Marching

mel - o-dy sweet-er than psalm; In ce - les - tial-like strains it un -
deep in the heart of my soul; So se - cure that no pow-er can
sweet-ly in Je - sus' con - trol; For I'm kept from all dan-ger by
Au - thor of peace I shall see, That one strain of the song which the
down the rough path-way of time! Make Je - sus your friend ere the

ceas - ing - ly falls O'er my soul like an in - fi - nite calm.
mine it a - way, While the years of e - ter - ni - ty roll.
night and by day, And his glo - ry is flood-ing my soul.
ran - somed will sing, In that heav - en - ly king-dom will be,
shad - ows grow dark; Oh, ac - cept of this peace so sub - lime.

CHORUS.

Peace! Peace! Wonder-ful peace, Coming down from the Fa-ther a - bove; Sweep

WONDERFUL PEACE.—*Continued.*

o - ver my spir - it for - ev-er, I pray, In fath -om-less billows of love.

61 LEND A HELPING HAND.

UNKNOWN.

J. BAPTISTE CALKIN.

Org.

1. "In his Name," my broth-er, Heart and hand u - nite; Pledg'd to love and
2. "In his Name," my broth-er, Heark-en to the call! Gird ye on the
3. "In his Name," my broth-er, Lift the fall - en one; Do the Master's

du - ty, Mer-cy, truth, and right. Join the ranks, now waiting, Hear his
ar-mor, Forward, one and all! Hearts there are in fetters, Ye can
bidding, As in heav'n 'tis done;— Cheer the faint and drooping, Help the
Cho.—Look - ing upward, outward, Vic - to-

sf *poco rit.* D. S.

kind command, Forward, brother! Forward! "Lend a help - ing hand."
break the band; On - ward to their rescue! "Lend a help - ing hand."
weak to stand; Forward, brother! Forward! "Lend a help - ing hand."
ry we'll gain, If we bat - tle no - bly In his bless - ed name.

67

62   O THOU GOD OF MY SALVATION.

THOMAS OLIVERS.

STEPHEN V. R. FORD.

1. O thou God of my sal-va-tion, My Re-deem-er from all sin;
2. Tho' un-seen, I love the Sav-iour; He hath brought sal-va-tion near;
3. While the an-gel choirs are cry-ing, "Glo-ry to the great I AM,"
4. An-gels now are hov-'ring round us, Un-per-ceived a-mid the throng;

Moved by thy di-vine com-pas-sion, Who hast died my heart to win;
Man-i-fests his pard-'ning fa-vor; And when Je-sus doth ap-pear,
I with them will still be vy-ing— Glo-ry! glo-ry to the Lamb!
Wond'ring at the love that crown'd us, Glad to join the ho-ly song:

I will praise thee, I will praise thee; Where shall I thy praise be-gin?
Soul and bod-y, Soul and bod-y Shall his glo-rious im-age bear.
O how pre-cious, O how pre-cious Is the sound of Je-sus' name!
Hal-le-lu-jah, Hal-le-lu-jah, Love and praise to Christ be-long!

I will praise thee, I will praise thee; Where shall I thy praise be-gin?
Soul and bod-y, Soul and bod-y, Shall his glo-rious im-age bear.
O how pre-cious, O how pre-cious Is the sound of Je-sus' name!
Hal-le-lu-jah, Hal-le-lu-jah, Love and praise to Christ be-long!

J. F.

JOSEPH FLETCHER.

Christ is ris-en! Christ is ris-en!

Cheer-ful - ly we sing the song; Christ is ris - en! Al - le - lu - ia! Ring the

bells, the strain prolong.

1. Mary came and sought the Saviour At the tomb where
2. O how pre-cious is the prom-ise If we seek him
3. If at last we sleep in Je - sus When he com - eth
4. Glory, glo - ry be to Je - sus—To the Lamb who

he had lain: But the ang-els told her tru - ly, "Je - sus Christ is ris'n a - gain.
we shall find; Find in him a friend and Saviour, Al-ways mer - ci - ful and kind.
we shall rise. And as-cend with him in tri-umph To our home in Par - a - dise.
once was slain; Christ, the king of earth and heaven, Ris'n for ev-er-more to reign.

69

64   HOW PRECIOUS JESUS IS TO ME.

S. V. R. F.   *Moderato.*

STEPHEN V. R. FORD.

1. How precious Je - sus is to me I can - not tell; but this I know,
2. He is my light, my joy, my rest; Whom shall I fear? No foe can harm;
3. Thro' Je - sus' all - a - ton - ing blood My soul is rid of ev - 'ry stain;
4. Till then I'll rest in Je - sus' love; The cross I'll bear, what-e'er it be,

That all is well, for I am free From sin and sor' - row, shame and woe.
While he is near, none can mo-lest, Nor pluck me from his might - y arm.
My life is hid with Christ in God, I shall with him in glo - ry reign.
That I may wear, in heav'n a - bove, The badge and crown of roy - al - ty.

REFRAIN.   *Andante.*

And when I join the ransomed throng, And learn the new ce - les - tial song,

Cres.

Rit.

I'll sing throughout e - ter - ni - ty How pre-cious Je - sus is to me.

UNKNOWN.

FRANK TREAT SOUTHWICK.

Voices in Unison.

1. Strains of mu - sic oft - en greet us, As we join the bus - y throng,
2. 'Tis a song of love and mer - cy, Speaking peace to all man-kind,
3. While we live, O may we ev - er Love this hap - py meet-ing song,

But there's noth-ing half so bright'ning, As our hap - py gath-'ring song;
Tell - ing broth-ers, poor and need - y, Where content-ment they may find;
And when death shall call us home-ward, Sing it with the heaven-ly throng;

ritard.

No fear of e - vil, no fear of wrong, While we sing our gath - 'ring song!
No fear of e - vil, no fear of wrong, While we sing our gath - 'ring song.
No fear of e - vil, no fear of wrong, While we sing our gath - 'ring song.

REFRAIN.—*Forte.*

Hal - le - lu - jah! Hal - le - lu - jah! Glo - ry be to God a - bove;

We can sing the wondrous sto - ry Of our Saviour's boundless love.

S. V. R. F.   STEPHEN V. R. FORD.

1. There is work for all, Both great and small, In the vine-yard
2. There is peace for all, Both great and small, In the pow'r of
3. There is joy for all, Both great and small, In the serv-ice
4. There is rest for all, Both great and small, In the Sav-iour's

of the Lord; And if we o-bey His call to-day, He
Je-sus' blood; Per-fect peace have they Who calm-ly stay Their
of our King; In the Ho-ly Ghost We make our boast And
boundless love; Soon the Lord will come And take us home To

CHORUS.

will our toil re-ward. There is work,   there is
hearts and minds on God. There is peace,   there is
songs of tri-umph sing. There is joy,   there is
reign with him a-bove. There is rest,   there is

there   is work,

Unison.

work,   There is work for all, Both great and small; There is
peace,   There is peace for all, Both great and small; There is
joy,   There is joy for all, Both great and small; There is
rest,   There is rest for all, Both great and small; There is

there is work,

THERE IS WORK FOR ALL.—*Continued.*

work,   there is work,   There is work for you and me.
peace,   there is peace,   There is peace for you and me.
joy,   there is joy,   There is joy for you and me.
rest,   there is rest,   There is rest for you and me.

There is work,   there is work,

67   ONLY TRUST HIM.

REV. J. H. S.   REV. J. H. STOCKTON. By per.

1. Come, ev - 'ry soul by sin oppress'd, There's mercy with the Lord, And he will
2. For Je - sus shed his precious blood Rich blessings to be - stow; Plunge now in-
3. Yes, Je - sus is the Truth, the Way, That leads you in - to rest; Be - lieve in
4. Come then, and join this ho - ly band, And on to glo - ry go, To dwell in

CHORUS.

sure - ly give you rest, By trusting in his word.
to the crimson flood That washes white as snow.
him with-out de - lay, And you are ful - ly blest.
that ce - les - tial land, Where joys immortal flow.

On - ly trust him, on - ly trust him,

On - ly trust him now; He will save you, He will save you, he will save you now.

73

THE CALL FOR REAPERS.

J. O. Thompson.

J. B. O. CLEMM.

1. Far and near the fields are teem - ing, With the waves of rip - ened grain;
2. Send them forth with morn's first beaming, Send them in the noon-tide's glare;
3. O thou, whom thy Lord is send - ing, Gath-er now the sheaves of gold,

Far and near their gold is gleam-ing, O'er the sun - ny slope and plain.
When the sun's last rays are gleam-ing, Bid them gath - er ev - ery-where.
Heav'nward then at evening wend-ing, Thou shalt come with joy un - told.

CHORUS.

Lord of har - vest, send forth reap - ers! Hear us, Lord, to thee we cry;

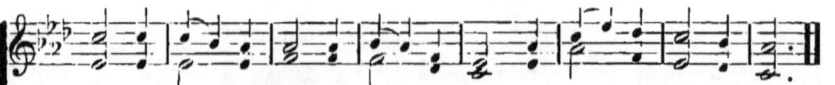

Send them now the sheaves to gath - er, Ere the har - vest-time pass by.

69 ## THE CHILDREN'S JUBILEE.

S. V. R. F.

STEPHEN V. R. FORD.

1. On this glad ju - bi - lee Let all the chil - dren raise Their
2. Je - sus, who sits en - throned In maj - es - ty on high, The
3. To God, whose watch-ful care Pro - tects us day by day, Whose
4. We join the heaven - ly host, As - crib - ing un - to thee, The

hearts and voic - es up to thee, O Lord, in songs of praise.
Christ who all our guilt a - toned, We laud and mag - ni - fy.
an - gels guard us ev - ery - where, We grate - ful hom - age pay.
Fa - ther, Son, and Ho - ly Ghost, All might and maj - es - ty.

REFRAIN.

Ho - san - na! Ho - san - na! Let all the chil - dren sing—

The glo - ries of Im - man - u - el, Ho - san - na to our King!

JOHN NEWTON.   FRANCIS JOSEPH HAYDN.

1. Glo - rious things of thee are spok - en, Zi - on, cit - y of our God;
2. See, the streams of liv - ing wa - ters, Springing from e - ter - nal love,
3. Round each hab - it - a - tion hov -'ring, See the cloud and fire ap - pear

He, whose word can - not be brok - en, Formed thee for his own a - bode;
Still sup - ply thy sons and daughters, And all fear of want re - move:
For a glo - ry and a cov -'ring, Show - ing that the Lord is near!

On the rock of a - ges found - ed, What can shake thy sure re - pose?
Who can faint while such a riv - er Ev - er flows our thirst t' as - suage?
He who gives us dai - ly man - na, He who list - ens when we cry,

With sal - va - tion's walls surround - ed, Thou may'st smile at all thy foes.
Grace, which, like the Lord, the giv - er, Nev - er fails from age to age.
Let him hear the loud ho - san - na Ris - ing to his throne on high.

PRECIOUS JESUS.

S. V. R. F.

STEPHEN V. R. FORD.

1. In the worth-y name of Je - sus, There is life and lib - er - ty;—
2. With th' an-gel - ic choir in glo - ry, And with all the saints in light,
3. Here, our pil - grim way pur-su - ing, Ere we cross the si - lent stream,
4. When the pearl-y gates we en - ter, And the King in beau-ty see,

Peace and com - fort, joy and glad - ness, For the soul from sin made free.
We the heirs of life im - mor - tal, In the Sav-iour's praise u - nite.
Je - sus' love shall be our rap - ture, Je - sus' name our loft-iest theme.
Je - sus' name we'll praise for-ev - er, In di - vin - est mel - o - dy.

REFRAIN.

Pre - cious Je - sus, Pre - cious Je - sus, Sweet-est name to mor - tals giv'n;

Pre - cious Je - sus, Pre - cious Je - sus, Name that thrills the hosts of heav'n.

STEPHEN V. R. FORD.

1. Peace in be - liev - ing, com - fort di - vine, Comes to my soul, since
2. Peace as a riv - er flows through my heart, Peace such as on - ly
3. Cast - ing my bur - dens all on the Lord, Trust - ing the prom - ise
4. Peace in be - liev - ing! whom shall I fear? Peace rules my heart since

Je - sus is mine; Trusting in him I find sweet re - pose, Peace such as
Christ can im - part; Gift of his mer - cy, gift of his love, Spir - it of
found in his word, Grace to sustain me free - ly is giv'n; Joy lights the
Je - sus is near; Bless - ed es - tate, from doubts I am free; Fore - taste of

on - ly Je - sus bestows.
heav'n sent down from a - bove. } Peace in believ - ing, com - fort re - ceiv - ing,
path - way lead - ing to heav'n.
bliss when Je - sus I see. }

REFRAIN.

Ful - ness of bless - ing, ful - ness of love; No gloom or sad - ness,

78

all joy and glad-ness, Prom-ise and fore-taste of heav-en a-bove.

73 MY PORTION FOREVER.

S. V. R. F.

STEPHEN V. R. FORD.

1. My por-tion for-ev-er, O Je-sus, thou art; My light and sal-
2. Whom have I in heav-en, dear Sav-iour, but thee? On earth there's none
3. Thrice bless-ed as-sur-ance, I know thou art mine! And so to thy
4. Dear Sav-iour, be with me, my Friend and my Guide, Thro' life's rug-ged

va-tion, the joy of my heart; In dan-ger my ref-uge, in
oth-er so precious to me; Thou art my com-pan-ion, my
pur-pose my all I re-sign; Con-tent e'en to suf-fer re-
jour-ney, what-ev-er be-tide; And when life is end-ed, O

dark-ness my guide, My rock and my fort-ress, in thee I a-bide.
love and my rest; Thy presence sus-tains me, in thee I am blest.
proach for thy name, Since thou hast re-deemed me from sor-row and shame.
then let me wear A crown in thy king-dom and reign with thee there.

OUR GLAD JUBILEE.

W. F. S.

WM. F. SHERWIN.

1. Wake, wake the song! our glad ju - bi - lee   Once more we hail with
2. March- ing to Zi - on, dear bless - ed home!   Lord, by thy mer - cy
3. Yet once a - gain the an - them re - peat,   Join ev - 'ry voice the

D.C.—*wake, wake the song! &c.*

FINE.

sweet mel - o - dy, Bringing our hymns of praise un - to thee, O most ho - ly Lord!
hith - er we come; Guide us, we pray where'er we may roam, Keep us in thy fear;
Mas - ter to greet: Love's sac-ri-fice we lay at his feet, In his temple now;

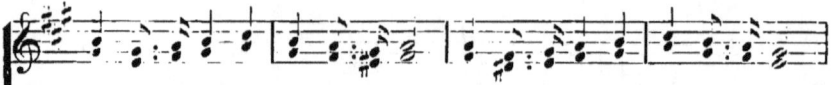

Praise for thy care by day and by night, Praise for the homes by love made so bright;
Fill ev - 'ry soul with love all di - vine, Now cause thy face up - on us to shine:
Je - sus, ac-cept the of-f'ring we bring, Blending with songs the o - dors of spring;

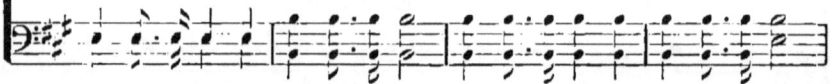

D.C.

Thanks for the pure and soul-cheer-ing light Beaming from thy word.
Grant that our hearts may tru - ly be thine All the com-ing year.
Still of thy won-drous love we will sing, Till in heav'n we bow.

CHO.—*Then*

75   **I'M NEARING HOME.**

(SUITABLE FOR A QUARTET.)

S. V. R. F.   STEPHEN V. R. FORD.

Moderato.

1. I shall be like my bless - ed Lord, For I shall see him as he is
2. Up - on the mount of faith I stand, And view with won-der and de-light
3. I catch the ech - o of the strain, The ransomed sing a-round the throne,
4. Since Christ is mine, and I am his, Ce - les - tial joys to me are giv'n,
5. In pa - tient wait-ing I'll a - bide, Till Je - sus comes my soul to take;

When I in-her-it my re-ward, In man-sions of e-ter-nal bliss.
The glo-ries of the Fa-ther-land, The cit-y hid from mor-tal sight.
And join them in the grand re-frain, As-crib-ing praise to Christ a-lone.
I an-te-date im-mor-tal bliss, And lin-ger on the verge of heav'n.
And then I shall be sat-is-fied, When in his like-ness I a-wake.

REFRAIN.

I'm near-ing home, I'm near-ing home, The pearl-y gates by faith I see;

And soon my Lord will bid me come To reign with him e-ter-nal-ly.

76   HAIL, THOU ONCE DESPISED JESUS!

(Tune: AUTUMN.)

JOHN BAKEWELL.

Spanish Melody from MARECHIO.

1. Hail, thou once de - spis - ed Je - sus! Hail, thou Gal - i - le - an King!
2. Pas-chal Lamb, by God ap-point - ed, All our sins on thee were laid:
3. Je - sus, hail! enthroned in glo - ry, There for - ev - er to a - bide;
4. Wor-ship, hon - or, pow'r, and bless-ing, Thou art wor - thy to re - cieve;

Thou didst suf - fer to re - lease us; Thou didst free sal - va - tion bring.
By al - might - y love a - noint - ed, Thou hast full a-tone-ment made.
All the heav'n - ly hosts a - dore thee, Seat - ed at thy Fa - ther's side:
Loud - est prais - es, with-out ceas - ing, Meet it is for us to give.

Hail, thou ag - o - niz - ing Sav - iour, Bear - er of our sin and shame!
All thy peo - ple are for - giv - en; Thro' the vir - tue of thy blood;
There for sin - ners thou art plead-ing; There thou dost our place pre - pare:
Help, ye bright an - gel - ic spir - its; Bring your sweetest, no-blest lays;

By thy mer - its we find fa - vor; Life is giv - en thro' thy name.
O - pened is the gate of heav - en; Peace is made 'twixt man and God.
Ev - er for us in - ter - ced - ing, Till in glo - ry we ap - pear.
Help to sing our Sav-iour's mer - its; Help to chant Im-man-uel's praise!

82

77

THE JOYFUL SOUND.

ISAAC WATTS. STEPHEN V. R. FORD.

1. Sal - va - tion! O, the joy - ful sound! What pleas-ure to our ears,
2. Sal - va - tion! let the ech - o fly The spa - cious earth a - round,
3. Sal - va - tion! O, thou bleed - ing Lamb! To thee the praise be - longs;

A sov-'reign balm for ev - 'ry wound, A cor - dial for our fears.
While all the arm - ies of the sky Con - spire to raise the sound.
Sal - va - tion shall in - spire our hearts, And dwell up - on our tongues.

CHORUS.

There's re - demp - tion full and free, In the Lamb for sin - ners slain;

There's re - demp-tion redemption.

There is life for you and me; Hal - le - lu - jah! A - men.

There is life, there is life

STEPHEN V. R. FORD.

1. When the tem-pest fierce is rag-ing, and the bil-lows o'er us roll;
2. Oft we ask how self - de - ni - als can pro-mote our fi - nal good,
3. What are all our bit - ter cross-es if we con-quer self and sin;
4. O the ec-sta-sy of meet-ing with the loved ones gone be-fore;

When the foe his war - fare wag-ing threatens to de-stroy the soul;
And we won - der how our tri - als prove God's lov - ing Fa-ther-hood;
What are all our earth - ly loss-es if the crown of life we win;
O the rap - ture of the greet-ing ov - er on the oth - er shore;

When the night-ly ter - ror meets us, and the ar - rows round us fly,
Still God's love our faith is woo-ing, and when faith is lost in sight
Tho' on beds of pain we lan-guish, tho' our tears be nev - er dry,
We shall see the King of glo - ry, we shall reign with him a - bove,

Je - sus' lov - ing mes - sage greets us, "Your re - demp - tion draw-eth nigh."
We shall know that he was do - ing for his chil - dren what was right.
We may sing in all our an-guish, our re - demp-tion draw-eth nigh!
While we sing the grand old sto - ry of re - deem-ing grace and love.

Look-ing up   toward the cit - y out of sight, Je - ru - sa-lem the
Look - ing up

gold-en, pre-pared for you and me; Look - ing up   toward the
Look - ing up

mansions fair and bright; Tho' now our eyes are holden, our home by faith we see.

79   THE LORD'S PRAYER. (*Chant*).

GREGORIAN.

1 Our Father who art in heaven, | Hallowed | be thy | name. ‖
  Thy kingdom come: Thy will be done in | earth, ·· as it | is in | heaven,

2 Give us this | day our— | daily | bread: ‖
  And forgive us our debts, as | we for- | give our | debtors.

3 Lead us not into temptation, but de- | liver | us from | evil; ‖
  For thine is the kingdom, and the power, and the glory, for- | ever. |
    A- — | men.

80 COME WITH REJOICING.

FANNY J. CROSBY. MRS. JOSEPH F. KNAPP.

March time.

1. Come with re-joic-ing, come with delight, Na-ture is wak-ing, glad and bright;
2. Guard-ed from danger, sheltered and blest, Un-der his ban-ner, calm, we rest,
3. O! what a Saviour, gra-cious to all, O! how his blessings 'round us fall;
4. Still may his mer-cy ten-der-ly flow, Still may he guide us here be-low;

Hearts o - ver-flow-ing gath-er to-day, Fill us with rap-ture, Lord, we pray.
Come we be-fore him, come with a song, Tell how he leads us all day long.
Gen-tly to com-fort, kind-ly to cheer, Sleeping or wak-ing, God is near.
Then when our jour-ney safe-ly is past May we be gathered home at last.

CHORUS.

Praise our Re-deem-er, tell of his love, Praise our Redeem-er, God a-bove.

Tell of his mer-cy, boundless and free, None can pro-tect us, Lord, like thee;

rall.

Tell of his mer-cy, boundless and free, None can protect us, Lord, like thee.

Copyright, 1882, by Joseph F. Knapp, By per.

86

1. Je - sus shall reign wher - e'er the sun Does his suc - cess - ive
2. To him shall end - less prayer be made, And end - less prais - es

jour - neys run; His king - dom spread from shore to shore, Till
crown his head; His name like sweet per - fume shall rise With

moons shall wax and wane no more. From north to south the
ev - ery morn - ing sac - ri - fice. Peo - ple and realms of

princ - es meet, To pay their hom - age at his feet; While western
ev - ery tongue Dwell on his love with sweet - est song, And in - fant

em - pires own their Lord, And sav - age tribes at - tend his word.
voic - es shall pro - claim Their ear - ly bless - ings on his name.

87

REV. G. W. BETHUNE.   C. C. CONVERSE. By per.

1. Come, let us sing of Je-sus, While hearts and ac-cents blend; Come,
2. We love to sing of Je-sus, Who wept our path a - long; We
3. We love to sing of Je-sus, Who died our souls to save; We
4. Then let us sing of Je-sus, While yet on earth we stay, And

let us sing of Je-sus, The sin-ner's on-ly Friend: His
love to sing of Je-sus, The tempt-ed and the strong: None
love to sing of Je-sus, Tri-umph-ant o'er the grave; And
hope to sing of Je-sus, Thro'-out e-ter-nal day; For

ho - ly soul re-joic-es, A - mid the choirs a - bove, To
who be-sought his heal-ing, He pass'd un-heed-ed by; And
in our hour of dan-ger, We'll trust his love a - lone, Who
those who here con-fess him, he will in heav'n con-fess; And

hear our youth-ful voic-es Ex-ult-ing in his love.
still re-tains his feel-ing For us a-bove the sky.
once slept in a man-ger, And now sits on the throne.
faith-ful hearts that bless him, He will for ev-er bless.

AT THE CROSS.

ISAAC WATTS.

R. E. HUDSON.

1. A - las! and did my Sav-iour bleed, And did my Sov-'reign die?
2. Was it for crimes that I have done, He groaned up - on the tree?
3. Well might the sun in dark-ness hide, And shut his glo - ries in;
4. Thus might I hide my blush-ing face, While his dear cross ap - pears;
5. But drops of grief can ne'er re - pay The debt of love I owe;

Would he de - vote that sa - cred head For such a worm as I?
A - maz - ing pit - y! grace unknown! And love be - yond de - gree!
When Christ, the might-y Mak - er, died For man the crea-ture's sin!
Dis - solve my heart in thank-ful - ness, And melt mine eyes to tears.
Here, Lord, I give my - self a - way, 'Tis all that I can do.

REFRAIN.

At the cross, at the cross, where I first saw the light, And the

bur - den of my heart rolled a - way;
rolled a - way;
It was there, by faith,

I re - ceived my sight, And now I am hap - py all the day.

By permission of R. E. Hudson, Alliance, O.

89

84 HE KEEPETH ME.

MARIAN FROELICH.

G. FROELICH.

1. My shield the Lord Je - ho - vah is, Since he is mine and I am his;
2. Clasped in his ev - er - last'- ing arms, I fear not Sa - tan's fierce a - larms;
3. Temp-ta-tions oft be - set my soul, And waves of sor - row o'er me roll;
4. And when I walk the riv - er's brink, I'll cross, nor 'neath the bil - lows sink;

What time I am a - fraid I flee To him, and then he keep-eth me.
For tho' my Lord I can - not see, I trust him, and he keep-eth me.
Still I can sing tri - um-phant-ly: The Lord, Je - ho - vah, keep-eth me.
For Je - sus shall my pi - lot be, Whose mighty arm now keep-eth me.

REFRAIN.

He keep-eth me, He keep-eth me, How safe am
keep - eth me, keep - eth me,

I, How strong is he; He keep-eth me, He keep-eth
keep - eth me,

me, O joy di - vine, He keep-eth me.
keep - eth me,

85   TELL IT TO JESUS ALONE.

J. E. RANKIN, D.D.

E. S. LORENZ.

1. Are you wea - ry, are you heav - y - heart-ed? Tell it to Je - sus,
2. Do the tears flow down your cheeks un - bid - den? Tell it to Je - sus,
3. Do you fear the gath - 'ring clouds of sor - row? Tell it to Je - sus,
4. Are you troub-led at the thought of dy - ing? Tell it to Je - sus,

tell it to Je - sus. Are you griev - ing o - ver joys de - part - ed?
tell it to Je - sus. Have you sins that to man's eye are hid - den?
tell it to Je - sus. Are you anx - ious what shall be to - mor - row?
tell it to Je - sus. For Christ's com-ing king - dom are you sigh - ing?

Chorus.

Tell it to Je - sus a - lone.
Tell it to Je - sus a - lone.
Tell it to Je - sus a - lone.
Tell it to Je - sus a - lone.

Tell it to Je - sus, Tell it to

Je - sus, He is a Friend that's well-known: You have no oth - er

such a friend or broth - er, Tell it to Je - sus a - lone.

C. C. CONVERSE. By per.

1. Broth-er, you may work for Je-sus; God has giv-en you a place In some
2. Broth-er, you may pray to Je-sus, In your clos-et and at home; In the
3. Broth-er, you may sing for Je-sus; O how pre-cious is his love! Praise him
4. Broth-er, you may live for Je-sus; Him who died that you might live; O! then

por-tion of his vine-yard, And will give sus-tain-ing grace.
vil-lage, in the cit-y, Or wher-ev-er you may roam;
for his bound-less bless-ings, Ev-er com-ing from a-bove;
all your ran-somed pow-ers To his ser-vice free-ly give;

He has bid-den you to la-bor, And has prom-ised a re-
Pray that he will send the Spir-it In-to some dear sin-ner's
Sing how Je-sus died to save you, How your sin and guilt he
Thus for Je-sus you may la-bor, And for Je-sus sing and

ward—E-ven joy and life e-ter-nal In the king-dom of your Lord.
heart, And that in his soul's sal-va-tion You may bear some hum-ble part.
bore, How his blood hath sealed your pardon,—Sing for Je-sus ev-er-more.
pray; Con-se-crate your life to Je-sus—Love and serve him ev-'ry day.

92

STEPHEN V. R. FORD.

QUARTETTE OR SEMI-CHORUS.

1. O   home to-night, yes, home to-night, Thro' the pearly gate and the o-pen door;
2. For the work is done and the rest begun, And the training time is for-ev-er past;
3. O the love and light in that home to-night, O the songs of bliss and the harps of gold;
4. O the joy that waits at the shining gates For the dear-ly loved far a-way, yet near;

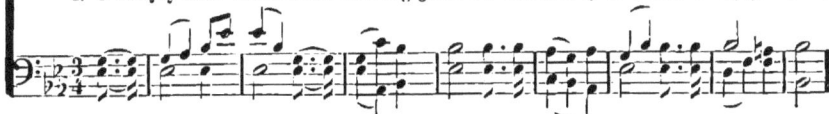

Some hap-py feet, on the gold-en street, Are en-ter-ing now   to go out no more.
And the home of rest, in the mansions blest, Is safe-ly and joyous-ly reach'd at last.
O the glo-ry shed on the new-crown'd head, O the telling of love that can ne'er be told.
When we all shall meet at his bless-ed feet In the light and love of   his home so dear.

FULL-CHORUS.

O home to-night, yes, home to-night, Thro' the pear-ly gate and the o - pen door;

cres.   rit.

Some hap - py feet, on the gold-en street, Are en-ter-ing now to go out no more.

93

88   JESUS, MY ALL, TO HEAVEN IS GONE.

(Tune: DUANE ST.)

JOHN CENNICK.   REV. GEORGE COLES.

1. Je - sus, my all, to heav'n is gone, He whom I fix my hopes up - on;
2. This is the way I long have sought, And mourn'd be-cause I found it not;
3. Lo! glad I come; and thou, blest Lamb, Shalt take me to thee, as I am;

His track I see, and I'll pur-sue The nar - row way, till him I view.
My grief a bur-den long has been, Be-cause I was not saved from sin.
Noth-ing but sin have I to give; Noth-ing but love shall I re-ceive.

The way the ho - ly prophets went, The road that leads from ban-ish-ment,
The more I strove a-gainst its pow'r, I felt its weight and guilt the more;
Then will I tell to sin-ners round, What a dear Sav-iour I have found;

The King's highway of ho - li - ness, I'll go, for all his paths are peace.
Till late I heard my Sav-iour say, "Come hither, soul, I am the way."
I'll point to thy re - deem-ing blood, And say, "Be-hold the way to God."

94

89   WHAT A MEETING THAT WILL BE.

T. W.

THEODORE WOOD.

1. When we all meet at home in the morn - ing, On the shore of that
2. When we all meet at home in the morn - ing, And from sor - row for -
3. When we all meet at home in the morn - ing, With our bless - ed, Re -

bright crys - tal sea; Where the loved ones who long have been wait - ing,
ev - er are free; When we join in the song of the ran - som'd,
deem - er to be; When we know and are known by our lov'd ones,

Cho.—Gather'd home,   gather'd

What a meet-ing indeed that will be!)
What a gath-'ring indeed that will be! }   Gather'd home,
What a meet-ing indeed that will be!)

home,   gather'd home,

gather'd home, On the shore of that bright crys-tal sea;

home,   gather'd home,

Gather'd home,   gather'd home, With our lov'd ones forever to be.

S. V. R. F.

STEPHEN V. R. FORD.

1. Christ is born! Christ is born! Clap your hands for joy! Ring the bells on
2. Je - sus lives! Je - sus lives! Clap your hands for joy! Par-don, peace and
3. Christ will come! Christ will come! Clap your hands for joy! He will take His

Christ-mas morn, Clap your hands for joy.
life he gives, Clap your hands for joy. } Clap your hands, Clap your hands,
chil - dren home, Clap your hands for joy.

REFRAIN.

Clap your hands for joy! Clap your hands, Clap your hands, Clap your hands for joy!

Copyright, 1891, by Hunt & Eaton, New York.

EDWARD PERRONET, alt.

OLIVER HOLDEN.

1. All hail the power of Je - sus' name! Let an - gels pros - trate fall;
2. Crown him, ye morn - ing stars of light, Who fixed this earth - ly ball;
3. Ye chos - en seed of Is - rael's race, Ye ransomed from the fall,
4. Sin - ners, whose love can ne'er for - get The worm-wood and the gall;
5. Let ev - ery kin - dred, ev - ery tribe, On this ter - res - trial ball,
6. O that with yon - der sa - cred throng We at his feet may fall!

Bring forth the roy - al di - a - dem, And crown him Lord of all;
Now hail the strength of Is-rael's might, And crown him Lord of all;
Hail him who saves you by his grace, And crown him Lord of all;
Go, spread your trophies at his feet, And crown him Lord of all;
To him all maj - es - ty as-cribe, And crown him Lord of all;
We'll join the ev - er - last - ing song, And crown him Lord of all;

Bring forth the roy - al di - a - dem, And crown him Lord of all.
Now hail the strength of Is-rael's might, And crown him Lord of all.
Hail him who saves you by his grace, And crown him Lord of all.
Go, spread your tro-phies at his feet, And crown him Lord of all.
To him all maj - es - ty as-cribe, And crown him Lord of all.
We'll join the ev - er - last - ing song, And crown him Lord of all.

92   CRUSADERS' HYMN.

UNKNOWN.   12TH CENTURY.

1. Beau-ti-ful Sav-iour, King of cre - a - tion, Son of God and Son of Man!
2. Fair are the meadows, Fairer the woodlands, Robed in flowers of blooming spring;
3. Beau-ti-ful Sav-iour, Lord of the na-tions, Son of God and Son of Man!

Tru-ly I'd love thee, Tru-ly I'd serve thee, Light of my soul, my joy, my crown.
Je - sus is fair-er Je - sus is pur - er, He makes our sorrowing spir-its sing.
Glo - ry and hon-or, Praise, ad-o - ra-tion, Now and for ev - er-more be thine.

THE KING OF GLORY.

(Tune, "EXALTATION.")

CHARLES WESLEY.
STEPHEN V. R. FORD.

1. Our Lord is ris-en from the dead; Our Je-sus is gone up on high;
2. "Loose all your bars of mas-sy light, And wide un-fold the e-the-real scene;
3. Lo, his tri-umph-al char-iot waits, And an-gels chant the sol-emn lay,

The pow'rs of hell are cap-tive led, Dragged to the por-tals of the sky:
He claims these mansions as his right, Re-ceive the King of glo-ry in!"
"Lift up your heads, ye heav'n-ly gates, "Ye ev-er-last-ing doors, give way!"

There his tri-umph-al char-iot waits, And an-gels chant the sol-emn lay:
"Who is this King of glo-ry? Who?" "The Lord, that all our foes o'er-came;
"Who is the King of glo-ry? Who?" "The Lord of glo-rious pow'r pos-sessed;

"Lift up your heads, ye heav'n-ly gates; Ye ev-er-last-ing doors, give way!"
The world, sin, death, and hell o'er-threw; And Je-sus is the conqueror's name."
The King of saints and an-gels, too, God o-ver all for-ev-er blest!"

KNOWLES SHAW.

GEORGE A. MINOR. By per.

1. Sow-ing in the morn-ing, sow-ing seeds of kindness, Sow-ing in the noon-tide
2. Sow-ing in the sunshine, sow-ing in the shadows, Fearing neither clouds nor
3. Go-ing forth with weeping, sow-ing for the Mas-ter, Tho' the loss sustained our

and the dew - y eve; Wait-ing for the har - vest, and the time of reap-ing,
win - ter's chilling breeze; By and by the har-vest, and the la - bor end-ed,
spir - it oft-en grieves; When our weeping's o - ver he will bid us wel-come,

CHORUS.

We shall come re-joic-ing, bring-ing in the sheaves.)
We shall come re-joic-ing, bring-ing in the sheaves. } Bringing in the sheaves,
We shall come re-joic-ing, bring-ing in the sheaves.)

Bring-ing in the sheaves, We shall come re-joic-ing, Bring-ing in the sheaves;

Bringing in the sheaves,   We shall come rejoic-ing,
      Bringing in the sheaves,   Bringing in the sheaves.

REV. THOS. J. POTTER.

STEPHEN V. R. FORD.

1. Bright-ly gleams our ban - ner, Pointing to the sky, Wav-ing wand'rers
2. Je - sus, Lord and Mas - ter, At thy sa - cred feet, Here with hearts re-
3. All our days di - rect us In the way we go; Lead us on vic-

on - ward To their home on high. Journeying o'er the des - ert,
joic - ing See thy chil - dren meet; Oft - en have we left thee,
to - rious O - ver ev - ery foe: Bid thine an - gels shield us

Glad - ly thus we pray, And with hearts u - nit - ed Take our
Oft - en gone a - stray; Keep us might - y Sav - iour, In the
When the storm-clouds lower; Par - don thou and save us In the

REFRAIN.

heav'n-ly way.
nar - row way. } Bright-ly gleams our ban - ner, Point - ing
last dread hour.

to the sky, Wav - ing wand'rers on - ward To their home on high.

100

96 HOME OVER THE SEA.

(MAY BE SUNG AS A QUARTET AND CHORUS.)

FANNY J. CROSBY. STEPHEN V. R. FORD.

Legato. *Vigoroso.*

1. On - ly a mo-ment of part-ing and tears, Then the sweet rap-ture of
2. On - ly the val-ley, the shad-ow, the stream, Then in its splen-dor the
3. There are the dear ones we miss from our side, An - gels have car - ried them
4. Still they are watching and wav-ing us there, On to their mansions so

Dim. *p* *Cres.*

in - fi-nite years; On - ly a whis-per, a ten-der fare-well, Then with our
morning's glad beam Breaks on our vis-ion with grandeur un-told, Fills with its
o - ver the tide; Now with the millions tri-umphant they sing, Cloth'd in the
love - ly and fair; Ties that were severed, a - gain we shall find, Hearts that were

f *Chorus.* *Andante.*

Sav - iour for - ev - er to dwell.
glo - ry the Cit - y of Gold.
like - ness of Je - sus our King.
brok - en, by friend-ship en - twined.

Home, home, o - ver the sea,
sweet

Dolce.

Beau - ti - ful E - den, our faith clings to thee; Home, home,
sweet

Rit.

o - ver the sea; Won - der - ful meet - ing, O what shall it be.

I LOVE THEE.

REV. JOHN A. GRANADE, 1800.   Arr. by HUBERT P. MAIN. By per.

1. I love thee, I love thee, I love thee, my Lord; I love thee, my
2. I'm hap-py, I'm hap-py, O wondrous ac-count! My joys are im -
3. O Je-sus, my Sav-iour, with thee I am blest! My life and sal -
4. O, who's like my Sav-iour? He's Salem's bright King; He smiles, and he

Sav-iour; I love thee, my God; I love thee, I love thee, and
mor-tal; I stand on the mount! I gaze on my treas-ure, and
va-tion, my joy and my rest! Thy name be my theme, and thy
loves me, and helps me to sing; I'll praise him, I'll praise him with

that thou dost know; But how much I love thee I nev-er can show.
long to be there, With Je-sus and an-gels, my kin-dred so dear.
love be my song, Thy grace shall in-spire both my heart and my tongue.
notes loud and shrill, While riv-ers of pleas-ure my spir-it doth fill.

GLORIA PATRI.

CHARLES MEINEKE.

Glo-ry be to the Fa-ther, and to the Son, and to the Ho-ly Ghost; As it was in the beginning, is now, and ev- er shall be, world without end. A-men, A-men.

99   LEAD, KINDLY LIGHT.

(Tune, "LUX BENIGNA.")

JOHN H. NEWMAN.   JOHN BACCHUS DYKES.

1. Lead, kindly Light, a-mid th' encircling gloom, Lead thou me on! The night is
2. I was not ev-er thus, nor prayed that thou Shouldst lead me on; I loved to
3. So long thy pow'r hath blest me, sure it still Will lead me on O'er moor and

dark, and I am far from home; Lead thou me on! Keep thou my feet; I
choose and see my path; but now Lead thou me on! I loved the gar-ish
fen, o'er crag and torrent, till The night is gone, And with the morn those

do not ask to see The dis-tant scene; one step e-nough for me.
day, and, spite of fears, Pride ruled my will. Re-mem-ber not past years!
an-gels fa-ces smile Which I have loved long since, and lost a-while!

THE MARCH TO VICTORY.

G. MOULTRIE.   C. C. CONVERSE. By per.

1. We march, we march to vic - to - ry, With the cross of the Lord be-
2. Our sword is the Spir - it of God on high, Our.... hel - met is his sal-

fore us, With his lov - ing eye looking down from the sky, And his
va - tion, Our... ban - ner the cross of Cal - va - ry, Our...

CHORUS.

ho - ly arm spread o'er us. } We come in the might of the Lord of light,
watchword the In-car - na - tion. }

A joy-ful host to meet him ; And we put to flight the ar-mies of night,

That the sons of the day may greet him.

3.
The choir of angels with song awaits
   Our march to the golden Zion ;
Our Captain has broken the brazen gates,
   And burst the bars of iron.

4.   [prove,
Then onward we march, our arms to
   With the banner of Christ before us ;
His eye of love looking down from above,
   And his holy arm spread o'er us.

J. MARSDEN.   STEPHEN V. R. FORD.

1. Go, ye mes-sen-gers of God; Like the beams of morn-ing fly;
2. Where the lof-ty min-a-ret Gleams a-long the morn-ing skies,
3. Go to many a trop-ic isle In the bo-som of the deep,
4. Where the gold-en gates of day O-pen on the palm-y East,

Take the won-der-work-ing rod; Wave the ban-ner-cross on high.
Wave it till the cres-cent set, And the "Star of Ja-cob" rise.
Where the skies for-ev-er smile, And th'op-press'd for-ev-er weep.
High the bleed-ing cross dis-play; Spread the gos-pel's rich-est feast.

REFRAIN.

Bear the ti-dings o'er the main; Tell the world sal-va-tion's free!

Christ the Lord is ris'n to reign! Hal-le-lu-jah! vic-to-ry!

THERE IS A GREEN HILL FAR AWAY.

Mrs. Cecil F. Alexander.   R. S. Willis.

1. There is a green hill far a-way, With-out a cit-y wall,
2. He died that we might be for-giv'n, He died to make us good,
3. Oh, dear-ly, dear-ly has he loved, And we must love him too,

Where the dear Lord was cru-ci-fied, Who died to save us all.
That we might go at last to heav'n, Saved by his pre-cious blood.
And trust in his re-deem-ing blood, And try his works to do.

We may not know, we can-not tell What pains he had to bear;
There was no oth-er good e-nough To pay the price of sin;
For there's a green hill far a-way, With-out a cit-y wall.

But we be-lieve it was for us He hung and suf-fer'd there.
He on-ly could un-lock the gate Of heav'n, and let us in.
Where the dear Lord was cru-ci-fied, Who died to save us all.

GLORY TO GOD.

FANNY J. CROSBY.

STEPHEN V. R. FORD.

1. Glo - ry to God, our strength and our Re-deem- er! Come with a song and
2. Lo, with his host he rid- eth on to con-quer, King-doms and crowns in
3. Glo - ry to God, the hope of ev - 'ry na - tion, Look un - to him and

wor-ship at his throne; He is the Lord, and there is none be - side him;
dust be- fore him fall; O clap your hands in joy- ful ex - ult - a - tion,
mag - ni - fy his name; Deep un - to deep shall tell of his sal - va - tion,

O spread abroad and make his wonders known.)
Lift up your voice, and hail him Lord of all. } Shout, shout aloud, ye ar-mies of the
Clime un-to clime his maj-es - ty pro-claim.)

REFRAIN.

faith-ful; Praise him who reigns our great and mighty King: Shout, shout aloud, the

ev - er - last-ing cho-rus, Let heav- en and earth with hal - le - lu - jahs ring.

MARCHING TO ZION.

Isaac Watts. REV. ROBERT LOWRY.

1. Come, ye that love the Lord, And let your joys be known, Join in a
2. Let those re - fuse to sing, Who nev - er knew our God; But chil-dren
3. The hill of Zi - on yields A thousand sa - cred sweets, Be - fore we
4. Then let our songs a-bound And ev - ery tear be dry; We're marching

song with sweet ac - cord, Join in a song with sweet ac - cord, And
of the heav'n-ly king, But chil - dren of the heav'n-ly king, May
reach the heav'n-ly fields, Be - fore we reach the heav'n-ly fields, Or
thro' Im - man-uel's ground, We're marching thro' Im - man-uel's ground, To

thus sur - - round the throne, And thus sur-round the throne.
speak their joys a - broad, May speak their joys a - broad.
walk the gold - en streets, Or walk the gold - en streets.
fair - - er worlds on high, To fair - er worlds on high.

thus sur - round the throne, And thus sur - round the throne.

CHORUS.

We're march - ing to Zi - on, Beau - ti-ful, beau - ti-ful Zi - on; We're

We're march-ing on to Zi - on,

march-ing up-ward to Zi - - on, The beau-ti-ful cit-y of God.

Zi - on, Zi - on,

105   LORD OF THE WORLDS ABOVE.

ISAAC WATTS.   STEPHEN V. R. FORD.

1. Lord of the worlds a - bove, How pleas-ant and how fair The
2. O hap - py souls, that pray Where God ap-points to hear! O
3. They go from strength to strength Thro' this dark vale of tears, Till

dwellings of thy love,.. Thy earthly tem-ples are! To thine a-bode
hap - py men, that pray... Their constant service there! They praise thee still:
each arrives at length, Till each in heav'n ap-pears; O glo - rious seat;

To thine a-bode

My heart as - pires, With warm de - sires To see my God.
And hap - py they That love the way To Zi - on's hill.
When God our King, Shall thith - er bring Our will - ing feet.

My heart aspires,

HOW FIRM A FOUNDATION.

(PORTUGUESE HYMN.)

GEORGE KEITH.   MARCOS PORTOGALLO.

1. How firm a foun-da-tion, ye saints of the Lord, Is laid for your faith in his
2. "Fear not, I am with thee, O be not dis-may'd, For I am thy God, I will
3. "When thro' the deep wa-ters I call thee to go, The riv-ers of sor-row shall
4. "When thro' fi-ery tri-als thy path-way shall lie, My grace, all-suf-fi-cient, shall

ex - cel - lent word! What more can he . say, than to you he hath said,
still give thee aid; I'll strengthen thee, help thee, and cause thee to stand,
not o - ver - flow; For I will be with thee thy tri - als to bless,
be thy sup - ply, The flame shall not hurt thee; I on - ly de - sign

To you, who for ref - uge to Je - sus have fled? To you, who for ref -
Up - held by my gra - cious, om - nip - o - tent hand, Up - held by my gra -
And sanc - ti - fy to thee thy deep - est dis - tress, And sanc - ti - fy to
Thy dross to con - sume, and thy gold to re - fine, Thy dross to con - sume,

uge to Je - sus have fled?
cious, om - nip - o - tent hand.
thee thy deep - est dis - tress.
and thy gold to re - fine.

5 "E'en down to old age all my people shall prove
My sovereign, eternal, unchangeable love;
And when hoary hairs shall their templesadorn,
Like lambs they shall still in my bosom. be
borne.
6 "The soul that on Jesus hath leaned for repose,
I will not, I will not desert to his foes;
That soul, though all hell should endeavor to
shake,
I'll never, no never, no never forsake!"

107 SPEAK JUST A WORD FOR JESUS.

S. V. R. F.

STEPHEN V. R. FORD.

1. Tell what the Lord has done for you, Speak just a word for Je - sus;
2. Ear - ly be - gin to bear the cross, Speak just a word for Je - sus;
3. Fear not the world nor heed its frown, Speak just a word for Je - sus;

Stand for the right, be firm and true, Speak just a word for Je - sus.
They who de - ny him suf - fer loss, Speak just a word for Je - sus.
They who en-dure shall wear the crown, Speak just a word for Je - sus.

REFRAIN.

Speak just a word, Speak just a word, Je - sus' a-bound-ing love pro-claim;

Glad - ly con-fess your ris - en Lord, Hon - or his ho - ly name.

108 MARCHING SONG FOR THE BOYS' BRICADE.

S. V. R. F.

STEPHEN V. R. FORD.

1. Fighting the bat-tles of the Lord, Marching to Zi - on, Marching to Zi - on;
2. Un - der the ban-ner of the cross, Marching to Zi - on, Marching to Zi - on;
3. Faithful to Je - sus on we press, Marching to Zi - on, Marching to Zi - on;
4. Je-sus will crown us at the last, Marching to Zi - on, Marching to Zi - on;

Armed with the weap-on of his word, March-ing to Zi - on's gates.
Glad - ly ac-count-ing all but loss, March-ing to Zi - on's gates.
Val - iant for truth and right-eous - ness, March-ing to Zi - on's gates.
When through the conflict we have passed, March-ing to Zi - on's gates.

REFRAIN.

Glo - ry to Je - sus our song shall be! Heav'n shall re-ech-o the mel - o - dy!

While we are march-ing to vic - to - ry, In our Re-deem - er's name.

109   WHEN JESUS LEFT HIS FATHER'S THRONE.

JAMES MONTGOMERY.   H. P. DANKS.

1. When Je - sus left his Fa-ther's throne, He chose an hum - ble birth;
2. Sweet were his words and kind his look, When moth-ers 'round him press'd;
3. When Je - sus in - to Sa - lem rode, The chil-dren sang a - round;

Like us, un - hon-or'd and un-known, He came to dwell on earth.
Their in - fants in his arms he took, And on his bo - som bless'd.
For joy they pluck'd the palms, and strow'd Their garments on the ground.

Like him may we be found be - low, In wis-dom's path of peace;
Safe from the world's al - lur - ing harms, Be - neath his watch-ful eye,
Ho - san - na our glad voic - es raise, Ho - san - na to our King!

Like him in grace and knowl-edge grow, As years and strength in-crease.
Thus in the cir - cle of his arms May we for ev - er lie.
Should we for - get our Sav-iour's praise, The stones themselves would sing.

Copyright, 1894, by H. P. Danks.

8

ON CANAAN'S SIDE.

S. V. R. F.

STEPHEN V. R. FORD.

1. On Ca-naan's side be - yond the tide Of Jor-dan's surg - ing riv - er,
2. No care they know, no pain or woe; No sor - row, grief or sad - ness;
3. Ful - ness of joy with - out al - loy— No more with sin con-tend - ing—
4. Life's conflicts past, they stand at last, With - in the shin - ing por - tal.

The ran-som'd stand, at God's right hand, Be - fore the throne for - ev - er.
There, free from sin, with Christ shut in, Their souls abound with glad-ness.
They share who meet at Je - sus' feet, And pleasures nev - er end - ing.
Where Je - sus is, en - throned in bliss, And wear the crown im - mor - tal.

REFRAIN.

In loft-y strains the praise they sing, Of Christ our prophet, Priest and King;

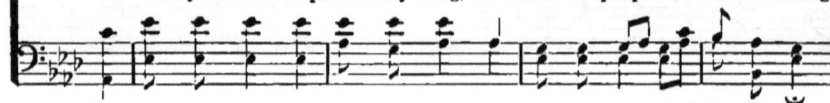

The Lord of glo - ry they a - dore, And wor-ship him for ev - er-more.

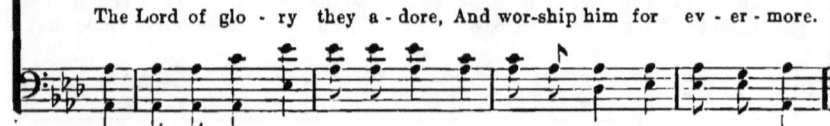

AN EVENING PRAYER.

JAMES EDMESTON.   STEPHEN V. R. FORD.

1. Sav-iour, breathe an eve-ning bless-ing, Ere re-pose our spir-its seal;
2. Tho' the night be dark and drea - ry, Darkness can-not hide from thee:

Sin and want we come con-fess - ing, Thou canst save and thou canst heal.
Thou art he who, nev-er wea - ry, Watch-est where thy peo - ple be.

Tho' de-struction walk a - round us, Tho' the ar - rows past us fly;
Should swift death this night o'ertake us And our couch be-come our tomb,

An-gel guards from thee surround us, We are safe if thou art nigh.
May the morn in heav'n a-wake us, Clad in bright and deathless bloom.

IN THE SAVIOUR'S STEPS I'LL FOLLOW.

E. Craft Cobern.

Frank Treat Southwick.

f Maestoso.

1. In the Sav-iour's steps I'll fol-low As I tread each pass-ing day, For his feet left
2. Jesus stooped to lift the fallen; Left his crown, forsook his throne And became for
3. On the lone-ly mount-ain kneel-ing, By the shore of Gal-i-lee, While the starlight

radiant footsteps As they pressed life's toilsome way. E'en the shadowed vale of sorrow
man a serv-ant, Wandered weary, scorned, alone. Saviour, I will seek a lost one,
fell in beau-ty, Je-sus prayed be-side the sea. Father, I will seek thy pres-ence,

rit.

Je-sus trod, for there I see Shin-ing, 'mid the mists and darkness, Footprints
I a staff of strength will be To some pil-grim, faint and trembling, Blindly
That this hu-man heart of mine May with thee, in sweet communion, Grow in

Chorus.
f a tempo.

he has left for me.)
grop-ing aft-er thee. } In the Sav-iour's steps I'll fol-low As I tread each
like-ness un-to thine.)

pass-ing day, For his feet left radiant footsteps As they pressed life's toilsome way.

113 KIND SHEPHERD OF THE SHEEP.

STEPHEN V. R. FORD.

JOHN HYATT BREWER.

1. Kind Shep - herd of the sheep, Who dost in safe - ty keep
2. Thou didst in days of old With - in thine arms en - fold
3. When dan - gers mul - ti - ply, If to thy side I fly,
4. Shep - herd di - vine, by thee Pro - tect - ed I would be,

Thy lit - tle flock; To thee my prayers as - cend; O let thine
A lit - tle child; O let me find a place In thy dear
By love in - clined— From sin's de - struc - tive charms, From Sa - tan's
While here I roam, And when I cease to rove, Ex - tend thine

ear at - tend My cry, be thou my Friend, My chos - en Rock.
arms of grace, Be - hold - ing there thy face, Be - nig - nant, mild.
fierce a - larms, Pro - tec - tion in thine arms May I not find?
arms of love To bear my soul a - bove To thy blest home!

REV. WM. HUNTER.   ARR. BY REV. J. H. STOCKTON.

1. The great Phy - si - cian now is near, The sym - pa - thiz - ing Je - sus:
2. Your ma - ny sins are all for-giv'n, Oh, hear the voice of Je - sus:
3. All glo - ry to the dy-ing Lamb! I now be - lieve in Je - sus;

He speaks the droop-ing heart to cheer, Oh, hear the voice of Je - sus.
Go on your way in peace to heav'n, And wear a crown with Je - sus.
I love the bless - ed Saviour's name, I love the name of Je - sus.

CHORUS.

Sweet-est note in ser - aph song, Sweet-est name on mor - tal tongue,

Sweet - est car - ol ev - er sung, Je - sus, bless - ed Je - sus.

4 The children too, both great and small,
    Who love the name of Jesus,
    May now accept the gracious call
    To work and live for Jesus.

5 Come, brethren, help me sing his praise,
    Oh, praise the name of Jesus;
    Come, sisters, all your voices raise,
    Oh, bless the name of Jesus.

6 His name dispels my guilt and fear,
    No other name but Jesus;
    Oh, how my soul delights to hear
    The precious name of Jesus.

7 And when to that bright world above,
    We rise to see our Jesus,
    We'll sing around the throne of love
    His name, the name of Jesus.

115 THE MASTER CALLETH THEE.

S. V. R. F.

STEPHEN V. R. FORD.

1. The Mas - ter is come, lo! he call - eth for thee; Give heed to his
2. The har - vest is great but the lab'rers are few; There's work to be
3. Let noth - ing de - ter thee, nor sunshine nor storm; Not e - ven an
4. For thee Je - sus call - eth, with all that thou art; Thy time, thine af-

summons, "Come, fol - low thou me; Why stand ye here i - dle? No
done which thou on - ly canst do; Go thrust in the sick - le and
an - gel thy task can per - form; Some sin - ner may per - ish for
fec - tions, thy tal - ent, thy heart; Thy sil - ver and gold on the

long - er de - lay, Go work in my vine-yard while yet 'tis to - day."
gath - er the sheaves: Who work-eth for Je - sus full wa - ges re-ceives.
ev - er and aye, Whose soul thou could'st rescue by work - ing to - day.
al - tar lay down; Give all to the Mas - ter, he'll give thee thy crown.

REFRAIN.

Call - - eth..... for thee,.......... Call - eth..... for
Call - eth for thee, for thee,   Call - eth for

thee.......... The Mas - ter is come, lo! he call - eth for thee.
thee, for thee;

116   SHALL WE GATHER AT THE RIVER?

ROBERT LOWRY.

REV. ROBERT LOWRY. By per.

1. Shall we gath-er at the riv - er Where bright an - gel feet have trod;
2. On the mar-gin of the riv - er, Wash - ing up its sil - ver spray,
3. Ere we reach the shin-ing riv - er, Lay we ev - 'ry bur - den down:
4. At the smil-ing of the riv - er, Mir - ror of the Sav-iours' face,
5. Soon we'll reach the sil - ver riv - er, Soon our pil-grim-age will cease;

With its crys - tal tide for-ev - er Flow-ing by the throne of God!
We will walk and wor-ship ev - er, All the hap - py gold - en day.
Grace our spir - its will de-liv - er, And pro - vide a robe and crown.
Saints whom death will nev-er sev - er Lift their songs of sav - ing grace.
Soon our hap - py hearts will quiv - er With the mel - o - dy of peace.

CHORUS.

Yes, we'll gather at the riv - er, The beau-ti-ful, the beauti - ful riv - er,—

Gath-er with the saints at the riv - er That flows by the throne of God.

117   CALM ON THE LISTENING EAR OF NIGHT.

E. H. SEARS.

STEPHEN V. R. FORD.

1. Calm on the list-'ning ear of night Come heav'n's me-lo-dious strains,..
2. Ce-les-tial choirs from courts a-bove Shed sa-cred glo-ries there; ...
3. The answering hills of Pal-es-tine Send back the glad re-ply; .....

Where wild Ju-de-a stretch-es far Her sil-ver-man-tled plains.
And an-gels with their spark-ling lyres, Make mu-sic on the air.
And greet, from all their ho-ly heights, The Day-Spring from on high.

REFRAIN.

"Glo-ry to God!" the sounding skies Loud with their anthems ring:......

"Peace on the earth; good-will to men From heav'n's e-ter-nal King."

4 O'er the blue depths of Galilee
  There comes a holier calm,
And Sharon waves, in solemn praise,
  Her silent groves of palm.

5 "Glory to God!" the lofty strain
  The realm of ether fills ;
How sweeps the song of solemn joy
  O'er Judah's sacred hills!

6 Light on thy hills, Jerusalem!
  The Saviour now is born:
More bright on Bethlehem's joyous plains
  Breaks the first Christmas morn;

7 And brighter on Moriah's brow,
  Crowned with her temple spires,
Which first proclaim the new-born light
  Clothed with its orient fires.

8 This day shall Christian tongues be mute,
  And Christian hearts be cold?
O catch the anthem that from heaven
  O'er Judah's mountains rolled!

9 When nightly burst from seraph-harps
  The high and solemn lay,—
"Glory to God; on earth be peace;
  Salvation comes to-day!"

BEAUTIFUL GATES.

Mrs. Margaret J. Preston.   C. C. Converse. By per.

1. Wea - ry the way the pil-grim goes, O - ver his path of sands—of snows;
2. What tho' the way be sometimes dark? If there be light e-nough to mark
3. Why should I build a - long the way Bowers of ease to tempt my stay?
4. Up! and be doing! the dusk may come, Ere I am more than half way home!

Still in his arms, thro' gain, thro' loss, Bear-ing the bur-den of the cross:
Just where the bleed-ing feet have trod, Showing the print of the Son of God?
Why should a pil-grim think to win Qui-et of heart in an earth-ly inn?
Storms that I wist not of, may rage O - ver my path of pil-grim-age;

Tar - ry - ing not thro' dark, thro' bright, Keeping my eye up - on the light,
Trustful, se-cure, I'll on - ward go, See-ing my Guide ap-points it so,
On - ly a lit - tle while to roam, On - ly a few short steps from home!
Yet on my heart the cross I'll bear (Lighter, the closer I hold it there!)

Chorus.

Far in the dis-tance, where I see
Trav'ling the path be-cause I see
Then, where the heav'nly man-sions be,
Joy - ful, for soon as the bourne I see, } Beau-ti-ful gates that o - pen to me;
Beau-ti-ful gates that o - pen to me;

BEAUTIFUL GATES.—*Continued.*

1 & 2. O-pen to me, O-pen to me, Beau-ti-ful gates that o-pen to me.
3 & 4. O-pen to me, O-pen to me, Beau-ti-ful gates will o-pen to me.

119 HAVE FAITH.

MISS A. STEELE.
Words of Chorus by CLARE.

C. C. CONVERSE. By per.

1. Ye wretched, hungry, starving poor, Behold a royal feast, Where mercy spreads her
2. See, Jesus stands with open arms; He calls, he bids you come; Guilt holds you back, and
3. Room in the Saviour's bleeding heart; There love and pity meet; Nor will he bid the
4. There, with united heart and voice, Before the heav'nly throne, Ten thousand, thousand

bounteous store For ev-'ry hum-ble guest.
fear a-larms; But see, there yet is room.
soul de-part That trembles at his feet.
souls re-joice In ec-sta-cies unknown.

CHORUS.

Have faith! have faith! Christ's

Have faith! have faith!

word of hope be-lieve; Have faith! have faith! Ask, and ye shall re-ceive.

Have faith! have faith!

123

120 SEAS ARE CALM AND SKIES ARE CLEAR.

FANNY J. CROSBY.   STEPHEN V. R. FORD.

1. Bless - ed Sav-iour! King of Glo - ry! Con - descend to dwell with me;
2. O 'tis joy to walk be - side thee, In the light of per - fect peace;
3. O the bliss that now is wait - ing, And the robe I soon shall wear;

Thro' this world of con-stant chang - es, Let my soul thy tem - ple be.
Joy to hear thee sweet-ly tell - ing Of a land where storms shall cease.
When the pal - ace gates I en - ter, And re-ceive thy wel-come there.

REFRAIN.

Bless - ed Sav - iour! King of glo - ry! All is well if thou art near;

Not a tho't of ill dis - turbs me, Seas are calm and skies are clear.

121   IN THY NAME, O LORD, ASSEMBLING.

(Tune: Sicilian Hymn.)

WALTER SHIRLEY.   MOZART.

1. In thy name, O Lord, as-sem-bling, We, thy peo-ple, now draw near:
2. While our days on earth are lengthened, May we give them, Lord, to thee:
3. There, in wor-ship pur-er, sweet-er, All thy peo-ple shall a-dore;

Teach us to re-joice with trem-bling; Speak, and let thy serv-ants hear:
Cheered by hope, and dai-ly strengthened, May we run, nor wea-ry be,
Shar-ing then in rap-ture great-er Than they could conceive be-fore:

Hear with meekness, Hear with meekness, Hear thy word with god-ly fear.
Till thy glo-ry, Till thy glo-ry Without cloud in heav'n we see.
Full en-joyment, Full en-joyment, Full and pure, for ev-er-more.

122   LORD, DISMISS US WITH THY BLESSING.

1 Lord, dismiss us with thy blessing,
  Fill our hearts with joy and peace;
Let us each, thy love possessing,
  Triumph in redeeming grace;
    O refresh us,
  Traveling through this wilderness.

2 Thanks we give, and adoration,
  For thy gospel's joyful sound;
May the fruits of thy salvation

In our hearts and lives abound;
  May thy presence
With us evermore be found.

3 So, whene'er the signal's given
  Us from earth to call away,
Borne on angels' wings to heaven,
  Glad the summons to obey,
    May we ever
Reign with Christ in endless day.
                WALTER SHIRLEY.

THE SPARKLING RILL.

UNKNOWN.   JAMES B. TAYLOR.

1. Gush-ing so bright in the morn-ing light, Gleams the water in yon fount-ain;
2. Qui - et - ly glide in their sil - v'ry tide, Pearl-y brooks from rocks to val - ley;
3. Touch not the wine, tho' it bright-ly shine, When a pur - er draught is giv - en;
4. O fountain clear, with a heart sin- cere We will praise thy glo-rious Giv - er;

And as pure-ly, too, as the ear-ly dew That gems the dis-tant mount-ain.
And the flashing streams in the strong sunbeams Like bannered arm-ies ral - ly.
A...... gift so sweet all our wants to meet, A bev-'rage bright from heav-en.
And.... when we rise to our na-tive skies, We'll drink of life's bright riv - er.

CHORUS.

Then drink your fill of the gush-ing rill, And leave the cup of sor - row;

Tho' it shines to-night in the gleaming light, 'Twill sting thee on the mor - row.

O COME TO THE SAVIOUR.

Arr. from J. HOPKINS.

D. C. JOHN.

1. O come to the Saviour, for why will you die, When God in his mer-cy is
2. Be-hold, he is wait-ing your souls to re-ceive, Re - ject him no lon-ger but
3. In rich-es and pleasure what can you ob-tain, To soothe your af-flic-tion or
4. O sin-ner, why starve and be feed-ing on air? Your Fa-ther hath plenty, e -

com - ing so nigh? Now Je - sus in - vites you, the Spir - it says "come," And
on him be - lieve; O per - ish - ing sin - ner, why will you not come, When
ban - ish your pain; To bear up your spir - it when summoned to die, And
nough and to spare, Distrust him no lon - ger, ac - cept him and see, And

Cho.—O come, come

an - gels are wait-ing to wel-come you home. ⎫
Je - sus is wait-ing to wel-come you home? ⎪
waft you to man-sions of glo - ry on high. ⎬ O come to the Sav-iour, and
prove that this mer-cy is boundless and free. ⎭

come..... .... O come come, come,..............

come to him now; O come to the Sav-iour, and come to him now, For

ritard.

an - gels are wait-ing to wel-come you home, to wel-come you home.

125   BY THY BIRTH, AND BY THY TEARS.

SIR ROBERT GRANT.

From KÜCHEN.
Arr. by STEPHEN V. R. FORD.

1. By thy birth, and by thy tears; By thy hu-man
2. By the ten-der-ness that wept O'er the grave where
3. By thy lone-ly hour of pray'r; By the fear-ful
4. By thy tri-umph o'er the grave; By thy pow'r the

grief's and fears; By thy con-flict in the hour Of the
Laz-a-rus slept; By the bit-ter tears that flow'd O - ver
con-flict there; By thy cross and dy-ing cries; By thy
lost to save; By thy high, ma-jes-tic throne; By the

sub-tle temp-ter's pow'r,— Sav-iour, look with pit-y-ing
Sa-lem's lost a-bode,— Sav-iour, look with pit-y-ing
one great sac-ri-fice,— Sav-iour, look with pit-y-ing
em-pire all thine own,— Sav-iour, look with pit-y-ing

eye; Sav-iour, help me, or I die (help me, or I die).
eye; Sav-iour, help me, or I die (help me, or I die).
eye; Sav-iour, help me, or I die (help me, or I die).
eye; Sav-iour, help me, or I die (help me, or I die).

126 ARE YOU ANCHORED?

FANNY J. CROSBY.

STEPHEN V. R. FORD.

1. Are you anchored on the Rock of A-ges? Are you hap-py in the Saviour's love?
2. Are you anchored on the Rock of A-ges? Are you seek-ing to re-claim the lost?
3. Are you anchored on the Rock of A-ges? On the Saviour have you cast your care?

Are you lean-ing on his arm of mer-cy, Ev-er look-ing for the joys a-bove?
Do you la-bor for the souls that per-ish, By the bil-lows and the tempest tossed?
Are you liv-ing for a home in glo-ry? Are your treasures and your heart all there?

REFRAIN.

Are you anchored, safe-ly anchored? On the Saviour's promise can you stand,

That for-ev-er he will hold you In the hol-low of his might-y hand?

9

127   MARTIAL SONG.

(For Epworth Leagues.)

Fannie J. Crosby.   Vivian Vincent.

1. Like an ar - my brave See our stand - ard wave, While the lost to
2. For the church we love, For our home a - bove, We our zeal to
3. While our toil we bear, O, what joy we share, While in fer - vent

save Forth we go;   O, how blest are we, Honored thus to be, Lord, to
prove All u - nite;   Swell our song of praise, While our hearts we raise, Here a -
pray'r Oft we bend;   Trusting God to bless We shall still pro - gress, And a

CHORUS.

spend for thee, Our days be - low.
mid the blaze Of gos - pel light.   On - ward, on - ward, where our du - ty calls us!
bright success Will crown the end.

Faint not, fear not, bold - ly march a - long.   On - ward on - ward,

shout - ing hal - le - lu - jahs, God is with us and our hearts are strong.

Copyright, 1894, by Hunt & Eaton, New York.

THOU ART COMING.

F. R. HAVERGAL.

C. C. CONVERSE. By per.

1. Thou art com - ing, O my Sav - iour! Thou art com-ing, O my king!
2. Thou art com - ing! thou art com - ing! We shall meet thee on the way;
3. O the joy to see thee reign-ing, Thee, my own be - lov - ed Lord!

In thy beau-ty all re - splen-dent, In thy glo - ry all tran-scend - ent,
We shall see thee, we shall know thee, We shall bless thee, we shall show thee
Ev - 'ry tongue thy name con - fess - ing, Worship, hon - or, glo - ry, bless-ing,

CHORUS.

Well may we re-joice and sing!)
All our hearts could nev - er say! } Coming! In the
Brought to thee with glad ac - cord!)

op - 'ning east, Her - ald brightness slow - ly swells!

Coming! O my glorious Priest, Hear we not thy golden bells?

W. Cowper. *"Redeemed * * * with the precious blood of Christ."—*1 Pet. 1:18-19. S. V. R. Ford.

1. There is a fount-ain filled with blood, Drawn from Im - man - uel's veins;
2. The dy - ing thief re - joiced to see That fount-ain in his day;
3. Thou dy - ing Lamb! thy pre - cious blood Shall nev - er lose its power,
4. E'er since, by faith, I saw the stream Thy flow - ing wounds sup - ply,
5. Then in a no - bler, sweet - er song, I'll sing thy power to save,

And sin-ners, plunged be - neath that flood, Lose all their guilt - y stains.
And there may I, though vile as he, Wash all my sins a - way.
Till all the ran-somed church of God Are saved, to sin no more.
Re - deem-ing love has been my theme, And shall be till I die.
When this poor lisp-ing, stamm'ring tongue Lies si - lent in the grave.

REFRAIN.

O the blood, the pre-cious blood, It cleans-eth me, It cleans-eth me!

pre-cious blood,

I am washed in the crim-son flood That flowed from Cal - va - ry.

HARK! THE SONG OF JUBILEE.

J. MONTGOMERY.

STEPHEN V. R. FORD.

1. Hark! the song of ju - bi - lee; Loud as might - y thun-ders roar,
2. Hal - le - lu - jah!—hark! the sound, From the cen - ter to the skies,
3. He shall reign from pole to pole With il - lim - it - a - ble sway;

Or the full - ness of the sea When it breaks up - on the shore:
Wakes a - bove, be - neath, a - round, All cre - a - tion's har - mo-nies:
He shall reign, when, like a scroll, Yon - der heavens have passed a - way:

Hal - le - lu - jah! for the Lord God om - nip - o - tent shall reign;
See Je - ho - vah's ban - ner furled, Sheath'd his sword: he speaks—'tis done,
Then the end;—be-neath his rod, Man's last en - e - my shall fall;

Hal - le - lu - jah! let the word Ech - o round the earth and main.
And the king-doms of this world Are the king-doms of his Son.
Hal - le - lu - jah! Christ in God, God in Christ, is all in all.

131   FOR MY SAKE.

UNKNOWN.   MENDELSSOHN.

1. Three lit - tle words, but full of sweet-est mean - ing, Three lit - tle
2. "For my sake" cheer the suff'ring, help the need - y: On earth this
3. "For my sake" let the harsh word die un - ut - tered, That trembles
4. "For my sake" press thou with all patience on - ward, Al - though the
5. And if in com - ing days the world re - vile thee, If "for my

words the heart can scarce - ly hold; Three lit - tle words, but on their
was my work, I give it thee; If thou wouldst fol - low in thy
on the swift, im - pet-uous tongue; "For my sake" check the quick re-
race be hard, the bat - tle long; With - in thy Fath - er's house are
sake" thou suf - fer pain and loss, Bear on, faint heart, thy Mas - ter

im - port dwell-ing, What ten - der - ness of love do they un - fold!
Mas - ter's foot-steps, Take thou and bear my cross and learn of me.
bell - ious feel - ing Which ris - es when thy broth - er does thee wrong.
ma - ny man-sions, There thine own voice shall join the vic - tor's song.
went be - fore thee, They on - ly wear his crown who share his cross.

132   CROSS AND CROWN.
                         (Tune: MAITLAND.)
GEORGE N. ALLEN, 1849.

1. Must Je - sus bear the cross a - lone, And all the world go free?
2. How hap - py are the saints a - bove, Who once went sorrowing here,
3. The con - se - crat - ed cross I'll bear, Till death shall set me free;

No, there's a cross for ev - ery one, And there's a cross for me.
But now they taste un - min - gled love, And joy with-out a tear.
And then go home my crown to wear, For there's a crown for me!

133   I WILL COME AGAIN.

S. V. R. F.

STEPHEN V. R. FORD.

1. If the world no joy af-ford, What so pre-cious then, As the prom-ise
2. They shall reap a blest re-ward Who have faith-ful been, Thro' the prom-ise
3. Bless-ed they who in the Lord Rest from toil and pain, Trusting in his
4. There is glo - ry in the word, "I will come a-gain!" E - ven so, O

REFRAIN.

of the Lord, "I will come a - gain."
of the Lord, "I will come a - gain."
faith - ful word, "I will come a - gain." } Com-ing, com - ing,
bless - ed Lord, Quick-ly come, A - men.

From his heav'n-ly throne; Christ is com - ing To re - ceive his own.

BLESSED ASSURANCE.

FANNY J. CROSBY.

MRS. JOSEPH F. KNAPP.

1. Bless-ed as - sur - ance, Je - sus is mine! O, what a fore-taste of
2. Per - fect sub - mis - sion, per-fect de - light, Vis-ions of rap - ture
3. Per - fect sub - mis - sion, all is at rest, I in my Sav - iour am

glo - ry di - vine! Heir of sal - va - tion, purchase of God, Born of his
burst on my sight, An - gels de-scend - ing, bring from a - bove, Ech - oes of
hap - py and blest, Watching and wait - ing, look - ing a - bove, Filled with his

CHORUS.

Spir - it, washed in his blood.
mer - cy, whis-pers of love.   This is my sto - ry, this is my
good - ness, lost in his love.

song, Prais - ing my Sav - iour all the day long; This is my

sto - ry, this is my song, Prais-ing my Sav - iour all the day long.

135   CHRISTIAN, DOST THOU SEE THEM?

ANDREW OF CRETE.
Tr. by J. M. NEALE.

J. G. BARNETT, Mus. Doc.

1. Chris-tian, dost thou see them, On the ho - ly ground, How the pow'rs of
2. Chris-tian, dost thou feel them, How they work with - in; Striving, tempting,
3. Chris-tian, dost thou hear them, How they speak thee fair? "Always fast and
4. "Well I know thy troub - le, O my serv - ant true; Thou art ver - y

QUARTET.

dark - ness Rage thy steps a - round? Chris-tian, up and smite them,
lur - ing, Goad-ing in - to sin? Chris-tian, nev - er trem - ble,
vig - il? Al - ways watch and prayer?" Chris-tian, an - swer bold - ly:
wea - ry, I was wea - ry too; But that toil shall make thee

Count - ing gain but loss; In the strength that com - eth By the
Nev - er be down-cast; Gird thee for the bat - tle, Watch, and
"While I breathe I pray!" Peace shall fol - low bat - tle, Night shall
Some day all mine own, And the end of sor - row Shall be

CHORUS.

ho - ly cross! In the strength that com - eth By the ho - ly cross!
pray and fast! Gird thee for the bat - tle, Watch, and pray, and fast!
end in day; Peace shall fol - low bat - tle, Night shall end in day.
near my throne; And the end of sor - row Shall be near my throne."

136   OUR BATTLE HYMN.

(For the Epworth League.)

MARIA GOODWIN PLANTZ.

JOHN HYATT BREWER.

f A la marcia.

1. Sol - diers start-ing for the bat - tle,   Let us work as one,
2. We will lift our com-rade's bur - dens,   Help-ing hands we'll lend:
3. Ho - li - ness is on our ban - ners,   Sin our on - ly foe;
4. For - ward then with great re - joic - ing,   For, the con - flict o'er,

That we may up-hold the stand-ard,   Of God's pre-cious Son.
And as one heart's earn - est plead-ings,   Shall our pray'rs as - cend.
And we can with strength u - nit - ed,   Sa - tan o - ver - throw.
We shall join the league of an - gels,   Who our King a - dore.

CHORUS.

We de - sire a league of - fens - ive,   To the pow'rs of sin;

To the cross of Christ de - fens - ive, And with God we'll win.

AUTHOR UNKNOWN.   STEPHEN V. R. FORD.

1. Lift the Gos-pel, ban-ner Wave it far and wide, Thro' the crowded cit - y,
2. Lift the Gos-pel standard, Spread the Gospel light; Let the bless-ed radiance
3. Let us rise to ac-tion, Work with one de-sign, Work with Christ and triumph

O - ver o-cean's tide: Sound the proc-la-ma - tion, Peace to all man-kind,
Flame o'er heathen night; Love is God's own sunshine, Such as an-gels prove:
In the work di - vine; Vic - t'ry's palm a - waits us, Let us then work on

REFRAIN.

Je-sus and sal - va - tion All the world may find.)
Conquer men by kind-ness, God himself is love. } Marching on to Zi - on,
Till we hear the welcome, "Faithful ones, well done!")

Soldiers of the King; With your shouts of tri - umph, Let the wide world ring.

138   HERALD ANGELS.

C. WESLEY.

FELIX MENDELSSOHN-BARTHOLDY.

1. Hark! the her - ald - an - gels sing, "Glo - ry to the new-born King;
2. Christ, by high - est heav'n a - dored, Christ, the ev - er - last - ing Lord;

Peace on earth, and mer - cy mild; God and sin - ners rec - on - ciled."
Veiled in flesh the God-head see; Hail, in - car - nate De - i - ty!

Joy - ful, all ye na - tions, rise, Join the triumphs of the skies;
Hail the heav'n-born Prince of peace! Hail the Sun of right-cous - ness!

With an - gel - ic hosts pro-claim, "Christ is born in Beth - le - hem;"
Light and life to all he brings, Ris'n with heal - ing in his wings;

With an - gel - ic hosts pro-claim, "Christ is born in Beth - le - hem."
Light and life to all he brings, Ris'n with heal - ing in his wings.

SWEET REST OF FAITH.

D. T. M.

REV. D. T. MACFARLAN.

1. I want a rest from ev - 'ry care, I want a life with thee to share, And
2. I want to live with perfect trust, Up - on thy prom-is - es so just, And
3. I come to thee, my bless-ed Lord, And sim-ply trust-ing in thy word, Lay
4. O peaceful rest! O bliss-ful love! Thy richest depths I ful - ly prove, And

prove thy faithful word; Thy rich-est grace in me ful - fill, And lead me by thy
true and right and good; With peace in God and strength in Christ, My living head my
all my burdens down; Close to thy bleeding side I rest, And find my soul su-
trust thy grace di - vine: I live with thee, thou liv'st with me, My life is hid with

Chorus.

per - fect will.
sur - est rest.
premely blest.
Christ in thee.

Sweet rest of faith, sweet rest of faith, Thy wondrous depths I fain would
[prove;

dim.

Sweet rest of faith, sweet rest of faith, Now fill me with thy per - fect love.

140 ARISE TO STRENGTH AND POWER.

Marian Froelich.

G. Froelich.

1. A - rise to strength and pow - er, To glo - ry all di - vine, Ye watchmen
2. Break forth in tune - ful meas - ures, Let loud ho-san-nas ring, Bring gems and
3. Hail him who comes in glo - ry, All hail the Prince of Peace! The Christ of

in the tow - er, Bid Zi - on rise and shine; No more in scorn-ful
jew - eled treas - ures, An offering to your King; When Zi - on's host re -
sa - cred sto - ry, Whose kingdom shall increase. Till ev - ery land be -

pit - y, Her foes de-ride her state, Glad psalms sweep thro' the cit - y, The
joic - es, Her foes are put to shame, While in her songs new voic - es Ex -
hold - ing, The splen-dor of the Sun Of righteousness, un - fold - ing, To

CHORUS.

A - rise and shine,

King is at the gate.)
alt the Saviour's name. } A - rise to strength and pow - er, He comes in might, in
Christ the Lord is won.)

ARISE TO STRENGTH AND POWER.—*Continued.*

A - rise and shine,

might and state; A - rise and shine, O Zi - on! Our King, our King is at the gate.

141 TO HIM WHO REDEEMS.

MRS. IDA M. BUDD. JOHN HYATT BREWER.

1. To him who re - deems and saves from de - spair, We bring humble
2. How best may we serve? in his word we find shown The du - ty of
3. We'll pray for our church, let our pray'rs nev-er cease, For her joy and pros -
4. At peace with man - kind, with our own hearts and heav'n, Our "right hand of
5. Thus firm - ly u - nit - ed for Je - sus we'll stand, In - spired by his

hearts fill'd with grat - i - tude's pray'r, And glad - ly con - fess that with
loy - al - ty each to his own; Our church is our joy and she
per - i - ty, com - fort and peace. We'll work while we pray, and our
fel - low-ship" e'er shall be given, To all who ex - alt as their
Spir - it, and led by his hand; We'll strive ev - er faith - ful - ly

serv - ice and song, Our lives thus re-deem'd to our Mas - ter be - long.
right - ful - ly claims Our tru - est en - deavors, our loft - i - est aims.
aim e'er shall be To win precious souls, blessed Sav - iour, for thee.
Sav - iour and Friend, The Christ our Re - deem-er, whose love hath no end.
on - ward to move, Till earth's toils shall cease and we serve him a - bove.

143

STAND UP, STAND UP FOR JESUS.

(Tune: WEBB.)

GEORGE DUFFIELD, JR.   GEORGE J. WEBB.

1. Stand up, stand up for Je - sus, Ye soldiers of the cross; Lift high his roy-al
2. Stand up, stand up for Je - sus, Stand in his strength alone; The arm of flesh will
3. Stand up, stand up for Je - sus, The strife will not be long; This day the noise of

ban - ner, It must not suf - fer loss: From vic - t'ry un - to vic - t'ry His
fail you; Ye dare not trust your own: Put on the gos- pel arm - or. Each
bat - tle, The next the vic-tor's song: To him that o - ver - com - eth, A

ar - my shall he lead, Till ev-ery foe is vanquished And Christ is Lord in-deed.
piece put on with pray'r; Where duty calls, or dan-ger, Be nev - er want-ing there.
crown of life shall be; He with the King of glo - ry Shall reign e-ter-nal - ly.

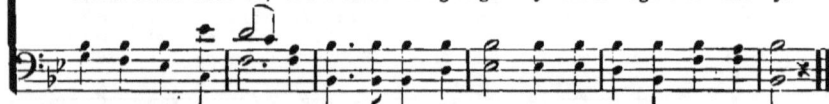

THE MORNING LIGHT IS BREAKING.

1 The morning light is breaking;
   The darkness disappears;
The sons of earth are waking
   To penitential tears;
Each breeze that sweeps the ocean
   Brings tidings from afar,
Of nations in commotion,
   Prepared for Zion's war.

2 See heathen nations bending
Before the God we love,
And thousand hearts ascending
   In gratitude above;

While sinners, now confessing,
   The gospel call obey,
And seek the Saviour's blessing,
   A nation in a day.

3 Blest river of salvation,
   Pursue thine onward way;
Flow thou to every nation,
   Nor in thy richness stay:
Stay not till all the lowly
   Triumphant reach their home:
Stay not till all the holy
   Proclaim, "The Lord is come!"

SAMUEL F. SMITH.

S. V. R. F.

STEPHEN V. R. FORD.

1. Lift up the ban-ner of the cross, Ye sol-diers of the Prince of Peace;
2. Close up the ranks! the trum-pet's blast Proclaims the hour of con-flict here;
3. The roy-al stand-ard is unfurled; Your Captain shouts the bat-tle-cry:
4. "Lo! I am with you," Je-sus saith, "Al-way!" O soul-in-spir-ing word!

The realm of sin shall suf-fer loss, While Je-sus' kingdom must in-crease.
In Je-sus' mighty strength stand fast, And give no heed to doubt or fear.
To arms! march on, and take the world, For Christ, who reigns enthroned on high.
Go out to bat-tle strong in faith, And dare to die for Christ the Lord!

REFRAIN.

Go forth re-solved in Je-sus' name, To con-quer in the dead-ly strife;

God's war-riors win im-mor-tal fame, And wear the star-ry crown of life.

10

THE ANGEL'S CAROL.

S. V. R. F.

STEPHEN V. R. FORD.

1. There was glad - ness in the song the an - gel sang—"Un - to
2. There was joy in heav - en a - round throne of light, When the
3. Wake the song of wel - come to the Prince of Peace, Waft the

you is born a Sav - iour, Christ the Lord;" O'er the fair Ju - de - an
cho - rus rang throughout the rift - ed sky; From the heav - en - ly host
joy - ful strain o'er ev - ery land and sea; 'Tis a song whose gold - en

hills the mu - sic rang, Till the list'n-ing earth the joy - ful ti - dings heard.
arrayed in garments white, Prais-ing God who reigns in maj - es - ty on high.
notes shall nev - er cease, Till the dawn of u - ni - ver - sal ju - bi - lee.

f CHORUS. p

Swell the cho - rus of the an - gel's joy - ful sto - ry,—Peace on

f

earth, good will to men! Peace on earth, good will to men! Swell the chorus, Glo-ry to the High-est, Glo - ry! Till the earth re - ech - oes o'er and o'er a - gain.

146   I BRING MY SINS TO THEE.

FRANCES RIDLEY HAVERGAL.   STEPHEN V. R. FORD.

1. I bring my sins to thee, The sins I can - not count, That
2. My heart to thee I bring, The heart I can - not read, A
3. I bring my grief to thee, The grief I can - not tell; No
4. My joys to thee I bring, The joys thy love has giv'n, That
5. My life I bring to thee, I would not be my own: O

all may cleans-ed be In thy once o - pen'd fount. I bring them,
faith - less, wand'ring thing, An e - vil heart in - deed. I bring it,
words shall need - ed be, Thou know - est all so well. I bring the
each may be a wing To lift me near - er heav'n. I bring them,
Sav - iour, let me be Thine ev - er, thine a - lone! My heart, my

Sav - iour, all to thee; The bur - den is too great for me.
Sav - iour, now to thee; That fixed and faith - ful it may be.
sor - row laid on me, O suf - f'ring Sav - iour, all to thee.
Sav - iour, all to thee, Who hast pro - cured them all for me.
life, my all I bring To thee, my Sav - iour and my King.

147   GOD BE WITH YOU.

Rev. J. E. Rankin, D.D.

W. G. Tomer.

1. God be with you till we meet a-gain; By his counsels, guide uphold you,
2. God be with you till we meet a-gain, 'Neath his wings protecting hide you,
3. God be with you till we meet a-gain, When life's perils thick confound you;
4. God be with you till we meet a-gain, Keep love's banner floating o'er you;

With his sheep se-cure-ly fold you,   God be with you till we meet a-gain.
Dai-ly man-na still di-vide you,   God be with you till we meet a-gain.
Put his arms un-fail-ing round you,   God be with you till we meet a-gain.
Smite death's threat'ning wave before you, God be with you till we meet a-gain.

CHORUS.

Till we meet,..... till we meet, Till we meet at Je-sus' feet;

Till we meet, till we meet, till we meet,   till we meet;

Till we meet,..... till we meet, God be with you till we meet a-gain.

Till we meet, till we meet, till we meet,

Copyright, by J. E. Rankin, D.D., Washington, D.C.

CONSECRATION.

MARY D. JAMES.   MRS. JOSEPH F. KNAPP.

1. My bod - y, soul and spir - it, Je - sus, I give to thee, A
2. O, Je - sus, might - y Sav - iour, I trust in thy great name, I
3. O, let the fire de-scend - ing Just now up - on my soul, Con-
4. I'm thine, O bless-ed Je - sus, Wash'd by thy cleansing blood; Now

con - se - crat - ed of - f'ring, Thine ev - er - more to be.
look for thy sal - va - tion, Thy prom - ise now I claim.
sume my hum - ble of - f'ring, And cleanse and make me whole.
seal me by thy Spir - it, A sac - ri - fice to God.

CHORUS.

My all is on the al - tar, I'm wait - ing for the fire:

Wait - ing, wait - ing, wait - ing, I'm wait - ing for the fire.

QUARTET & CHORUS.

1. Toil - ing in vain through the night dark and dreary, Seek-ing to res-cue some
2. If thou art wea - ry and faint in well do-ing, Gird on the ar - mor a -
3. Christ, for the joy set be - fore him in heav-en, Suf-fered to res-cue thy
4. Why should the Mas-ter thy toil be en-treat-ing? Hast thou no faith in the

soul from de - spair; Toil-ing in vain, till the heart, faint and wea- ry,
new for thy toil; He who with mal - ice the lost is pur - su - ing,
soul from the grave; Free-ly his life for thy ran-som was giv-en—
prom-ised re - ward? On - ly the faith-ful shall hear the glad greet-ing:

CHORUS.

Sinks 'neath its bur - den of toil, doubt and care.)
Suf - fers no fail - ure his pur - pose to foil. |
Wilt thou not la - bor an - oth - er to save? { Cour-age, my brother! the
"En - ter thou in - to the joy of thy Lord!")

Mas-ter is say-ing, "Cast in the net at my bid-ding a - gain;" Doubt not, nor

150

fal - ter, the Sav - iour o - bey-ing, Thou shalt no lon-ger be toil-ing in vain.

150   GRANT US THY PEACE. (Parting Hymn.)

JOHN ELLERTON.   STEPHEN V. R. FORD.

1. Sav - iour, a - gain to thy dear name we raise, With one ac -
2. Grant us thy peace up - on our home-ward way; With thee be -
3. Grant us thy peace, Lord, thro' the com - ing night; Turn thou for
4. Grant us thy peace through-out our earth - ly life, Our balm in

cord, our part - ing hymn of praise; We stand to bless thee
gan, with thee shall end the day: Guard thou the lips from
us its dark - ness in - to light; From harm and dan - ger
sor - row, and our stay in strife; Then, when thy voice shall

ere our worship cease, Then, low - ly kneel - ing, wait thy word of peace.
sin, the hearts from shame, That in this house have called up - on thy name.
keep thy chil-dren free, For dark and light are both a - like to thee.
bid our con-flict cease, Call us, O Lord, to thine e - ter - nal peace.

YIELD NOT TO TEMPTATION.

H. R. Palmer.   H. R. Palmer. By per.

1. Yield not to temp-ta-tion, For yield-ing is sin, Each vic-t'ry will
2. Shun e-vil com-pan-ions, Bad language dis-dain, God's name hold in
3. To him that o'er-com-eth God giv-eth a crown, Thro' faith we shall

help you Some oth-er to win; Fight man-ful-ly on-ward,
rev-'rence, Nor take it in vain; Be thought-ful and earn-est,
con-quer, Though oft-en cast down; He who is our Sav-iour,

Dark passions sub-due, Look ev-er to Je-sus, He'll car-ry you through.
Kind-heart-ed and true, Look ev-er to Je-sus, He'll car-ry you through.
Our strength will re-new, Look ev-er to Je-sus, He'll car-ry you through.

Chorus.

Ask the Sav-iour to help you, Com-fort, strengthen, and keep you:

He is will-ing to aid you, He will car-ry you through.

SOLDIERS OF THE CROSS.

(SUITABLE FOR THE BOYS' BRIGADE.)

S. V. R. F.

STEPHEN V. R. FORD.

Not too fast

1. We are sol-diers of the cross, marching on to Zi-on's gates, Millions
2. We will bat-tle for the right in the ar - my of the Lord, And the
3. Trusting in the Lord of Hosts, tho' the con-flict may be long, We shall

gone before have won the victor's crown; In the New Je-ru - salem, Christ, the
cause of truth and righteousness defend; Naught shall harm us if we trust in the
con-quer—Zi-on's warriors ne'er retreat—Here we fight the fight of faith, there we'll

REFRAIN.

King of Glory, waits To receive us when we lay our ar-mor down. } [shall
prom-ise of his word: I am with you alway, e-ven to the end. } And our battle-cry
sing the victor's song, When we lay our trophies down at Jesus' feet }

be, Christ the Lord and vic-tory, In his worthy name we'll triumph, tho' we die. We shall

conquer in the strife, We shall win the crown of life, And with Jesus reign forever in the sky.

HE HAS COME.

MRS. J. H. KNOWLES.

MRS. JOSEPH F. KNAPP.

1. He has come! he has come! my Re-deem-er has come, He has
2. He has come! he has come! my Love and my Lord, Ev-ery
3. He has come! he has come! O hap-pi-est heart, He has
4. He has come to a-bide, and ho-ly must be The

tak-en my heart as his own chos-en home; At last I have giv-en the
tho't of my be-ing is swayed by his word; He has come! and he rules in the
giv-en his word that he will not de-part; No troub-le can en-ter, no
place where my Lord deigns to banquet with me; And this is my pray'r, Lord,

wel-come he sought, He has come and his com-ing all glad-ness has brought.
realms of my soul, And his scep-ter is love, O bless-ed con-trol!
e-vil can come, To the heart where the God of peace has his home.
since thou art come, Make meet for thy presence my heart as thy home.

CHORUS.

Joy! joy is mine, My Sav-iour di-vine, Comes to a-bide with me, with me,

with me,

Comes to a-bide, ev-er to a-bide, My own lov-ing Saviour a-bid-eth with me.

STEPHEN V. R. FORD.

1. The Lord has giv-en me a precious song, A song of joy di-vine;
2. I knelt in sor-row at the mer-cy seat, And sought the Lord in pray'r;
3. He spoke my sins for-giv-en, and I rose From condemna-tion free;
4. And now a-mid the din of earth-ly strife, The song which he has given,

It thrills my soul with rapture all day long: "Je-sus, the Lord, is mine!"
His word of prom-ise told me I should meet My dear Re-deem-er there.
And now I tri-umph ov-er all my foes, Thro' Christ, who dwells in me:
Is the sweet fore-taste of im-mor-tal life, With Christ, my Lord, in heav'n.

REFRAIN.

O rapt'rous song, thy mel-o-dy In life and death my joy shall be;

I'll sing throughout e-ter-ni-ty, "Je-sus, the Lord, is mine!"

155

155   LORD, IN MERCY HEAR US.

REV. T. B. POLLOCK.   C. C. CONVERSE. By per.

1. Je - sus, we are far a - way From the light of heav'n-ly day,
2. On our dark - ness shed thy light, Lead our wills to what is right,
3. May the world seem on - ly dross, May we wel-come shame and loss,
4. May thy grace with - in the soul Na - ture's way-ward - ness con - trol,

Lost in paths of sin we stray; Lord, in mer - cy hear us.
Wash our e - vil na - ture white; Lord, in mer - cy hear us.
Will - ing - ly en - dure the cross; Lord, in mer - cy hear us.
Guid - ing tow'rds the heav'n - ly goal; Lord, in mer - cy hear us.

Deep - er has the dark-ness grown; Sav - iour, come to seek thine own.
May thy wis - dom be our guide, Com - fort, rest, and peace pro - vide
When oppressed with troub - le sore, Teach our hearts to feel the more
So at last, from sin set free, What we long for may we see,

Leave, oh, leave us not a - lone; Lord in mer - cy hear us.
Near to thy pro - tect - ing side; Lord in mer - cy hear us.
For the pangs our Sav - iour bore; Lord in mer - cy hear us.
And for ev - er bless - ed be; Lord in mer - cy hear us.

156   I'LL CROSS THE RIVER SINGING.

S. V. R. F.

Stephen V. R. Ford.

1. I love the song the ransomed sing—Re - deem - ing love the sto - ry—
2. The song that fills the heav'n-ly choir With ho - ly ad - o - ra - tion,
3. Be - fore the throne the ransomed stand, Ar - rayed in re - gal splen-dor;
4. And when the heav'n - ly host I meet, Be - yond the shin - ing por - tal,

As - crib - ing praise to Christ, our King, Who reigns en-throned in glo - ry.
They learned while passing thro' the fire, Of earth - ly trib - u - la - tion.
They take their crowns from Je - sus' hand, And end - less prais - es ren - der.
I'll sing re - deem - ing love, and greet Je - sus, the King im-mor - tal.

REFRAIN.

Love shall in - spire my lat - est breath, While to the cross I'm cling - ing;

The theme shall thrill my soul in death, I'll cross the riv - er sing - ing.

B. BARTON.
ROBERT PAYSON.

1. Walk in the light! so shalt thou know That fellowship of love, His spir - it
2. Walk in the light! and thou shalt find Thy heart made truly his, Who dwells in
3. Walk in the light! and thou shalt own Thy darkness passed away, Be - cause that
4. Walk in the light! and e'en the tomb No fearful shade shall wear; Glo - ry shall
5. Walk in the light! thy path shall be Peaceful, serene and bright; For God by

REFRAIN.

on - ly can be-stow Who reigns in light a - bove.
cloudless light enshrined, In whom no dark-ness is.
light hath on thee shone, In which is per-fect day.
chase a-way its gloom, For Christ hath conquered there.
grace shall dwell in thee, And God him-self is light.

} O, the precious light, shining

clear and bright, I am walk-ing in the light of God; I am
in the light of God;

cleansed from sin, I have peace within, Thro' the Saviour's all - a - ton - ing blood.

158

158

S. V. R. F.

REDEMPTION IN JESUS.

STEPHEN V. R. FORD.

1. There is life and sal - va - tion In the cru - ci - fied One:
2. There is free - dom in Je - sus From the an - guish of sin:
3. He hath car - ried our sor - rows, All our griefs he hath borne,
4. Christ is wait - ing in glo - ry, For the faith - ful who come

There is hope in God's mer - cy Thro' the blood of his Son.
With his par - don he giv - eth Joy and glad - ness with - in.
And his pro - mise as - sures us, They are bless - ed that mourn.
Out of great trib - u - la - tion, To their heav - en - ly home.

REFRAIN.

There's re - demp - tion in Je - sus, Swell the joy - ful re - frain!

There's re - demp - tion in Je - sus, Hal - le - lu - jah! A - men!

159 SOON MAY THE LAST GLAD SONG ARISE.

(Tune: MIGDOL.)

MRS. VOKE.

LOWELL MASON.

1. Soon may the last glad song a - rise, Thro' all the mill - ions of the skies;
2. Let thrones and pow'rs and kingdoms be O - be - dient, might - y God, to thee;
3. O let that glorious anthem swell; Let host to host the tri - umph tell,

That song of triumph which re - cords That all the earth is now the Lord's.
And over land and stream and main, Now wave the scep - ter of thy reign.
Till not one reb - el heart re - mains, But o - ver all the Sav - iour reigns.

160 I AM TRUSTING, LORD, IN THEE.

WILLIAM McDONALD.

WILLIAM G. FISCHER.

1. I am com - ing to the cross; I am poor and weak and blind;
2. Long my heart has sigh'd for thee, Long has e - vil reign'd with - in;
3. In thy prom - is - es I trust; Now I feel the blood ap - plied;
Cho.—I am trust - ing, Lord, in thee, Dear.. Lamb of Cal - va - ry;

I am count - ing all but dross; I shall full sal - va - tion find.
Je - sus sweet - ly speaks to me, I will cleanse you from all sin.
I am pros - trate in the dust; I with Christ am cru - ci - fied.
Humbly at thy cross I bow— Save me, Je - sus, save me now.

THROW OPEN THE GATES.

(Isaiah 26. 2.)

L. E. Jones.   W. S. Nickle.

1. Throw o - pen the gates of the cit - y, The cit - y of
2. Throw o - pen the gates of the cit - y, The cit - y of
3. Throw o - pen the gates of the cit - y, Let it's glo - ry shine

crys - tal and gold, That all who ac - cept of the Sav - iour May
joy and of love, That its light may shine out on the path - way That
out like a star, That the mill - ions who know not the Sav - iour May

CHORUS.

en - ter with joy to the fold.
leads to bright man-sions a - bove. } Throw o - pen the gates of the
hast - en from near and a - far.

cit - y, That its light may shine out on the way; Throw o - pen the

gates of the cit - y, We are near - ing its por - tals to - day.

11   161

THE CITY OF GOLD.

S. V. R. F.

STEPHEN V. R. FORD.

1. I seek for a cit-y whose builder is God, Whose street, bright and golden, no
2. No sickness shall en-ter the cit-y of life; No sor-row nor sighing, no
3. The saints shall not fear for the ter-ror by night, Nor the ar-row by day in the
4. No sin e'er shall en-ter the cit-y of peace; Con-ten-tion and ha-tred for-

mor-tal hath trod; Its walls are of jas-per, its gates pearl-y white, And
pain and no strife, No part-ing with loved ones, no tear-ful good-bye Shall
cit-y of light; No harm shall be-fall them, what-ev-er be-tide, Who
ev-er shall cease; All dis-cords re-solve in-to har-mo-ny sweet, And

God is its tem-ple, Mes-si-ah its light.
ev-er em-bit-ter the home in the sky.
un-der the in-fi-nite shad-ow a-bide.
love blend all souls at Im-man-u-el's feet.

REFRAIN.

The King in his beau-ty mine

eyes shall be-hold, With maj-es-ty crowned in the Cit-y of Gold; In songs of glad

triumph his praises I'll sing, As-crib-ing all glo-ry to Je-sus, my King.

O, LET US BE GLAD.

VINNIE VERNON.

T. FRANK ALLEN.

1. Oh, let us be glad in our Sav-iour and King, No tongues ev-er
2. His won-der-ful name makes our vic-to-ry sure, We share in his
3. We bless his dear name through smiles and through tears, His love all the

had great-er rea-son to sing, Our hearts we will raise with our voic-es in
fame, which shall ev-er en-dure; On earth we've his word and the gift of his
same hath encompassed our years; Oh who could be sad when thus held in his

Cho.—Be glad............ be

song, And give him the praise to whom praises belong.)
love; The joy of the Lord yet a-waits us a-bove. } Be glad, oh, be glad be
care, Come, let us be glad, and God's goodness declare.)

glad,..................

glad, oh, be glad; Oh, let us be glad in our King;......... Lift
King, in our King;

shall ring ...

up hap-py voic-es and praise him, Till space with his praises, his praises shall ring,

shall ring,.......

164   THE GLORY LAND.

Isaac Watts.   Ralph W. Pruyn.

1. There   is   a land of   pure de-light, Where saints im-mor-tal   reign;
2. There   ev - er - last - ing spring a-bides, And nev-er-with' - ring flowers;
3. Sweet   fields be-yond the   swell-ing flood, Stand dressed in liv - ing green;
4. Could   we but climb where   Moses stood, And view the land-scape   o'er,

In - fi - nite day ex - cludes the night, And pleasures ban-ish   pain.
Death, like a nar - row   sea, di - vides This heav'nly land from ours.
So   to the Jews old   Ca-naan stood, While Jor-dan rolled be - tween.
Not   Jor-dan's stream, nor death's cold flood, Should fright us from the shore.

REFRAIN.

O the   land   the glo - ry land, Where the wea-ry are at   rest;
glo - ry land,

There we all shall meet at Je - sus' feet, And be for - ev - er blest.

MARY J. ALLERTON.   EZRA D. YOUNG.

1. Be - cause my mind is stayed on God, In per - fect peace he keeps me;
2. A - mid the din of earth - ly strife, In per - fect peace he keeps me;
3. When waves of sor - row round me roll, In per - fect peace he keeps me;
4. In life, in death, I'll fear no ill,— In per - fect peace he keeps me;

I trust in Christ's a - ton - ing blood, In per - fect peace he keeps me.
His pres - ence sweet-ens all my life, In per - fect peace he keeps me.
He lifts all bur - dens from my soul, In per - fect peace he keeps me.
My feet shall stand on Zi - on's hill,— In per - fect peace he keeps me.

REFRAIN.

Peace,   peace! per - fect peace! Hal - le - lu - jah to the Lord!
Peace, sweet

166   HAVE YOU HEARD THE INVITATION?

S. V. R. F.

STEPHEN V. R. FORD.

1. Have you heard the in - vi - ta - tion   Of the Spir - it and the Bride?
2. Hast - en forth, O do not tar - ry!   Stay not! heed the Lord's be - hest!
3. Go, the love of Christ re-veal - ing;   To the cross the sin - sick guide;
4. Je - sus saith, "Let him that hear - eth   Shout the in - vi - ta - tion, 'Come!'"

Are you trust-ing for sal - va - tion   In the Sav-iour cru - ci - fied?
To the lost the ti - dings car - ry,   "Come, and Christ will give you rest."
Point them to the Fount of heal - ing   Flowing from the Saviour's side.
Go! and when the Lord ap - pear - eth,   He will guide you safe - ly home.

REFRAIN.

Go, re - peat the wondrous sto - ry,   To the world the mes - sage give;

"Come to Christ, the Lord of glo - ry,   Come, O come to Christ and live."

167 SINNER, WHAT SAY YOU?

GENEVA G. MOORE.

REV. SAMUEL ALMAN.

1. One more day is dy-ing In the dis-ant west: Are we one day near-er,
2. Re-veil-le has sound-ed At the ear-ly dawn, Calling us to du-ty;
3. When life's war is end-ed, And the set-ting sun Marks our last day's bat-tle,

To that land of rest? What has been our rec-ord? What good have we done?
Now the day is done—As we light our camp-fires 'Neath the fall-ing dew,
And we're go-ing home, What will be our greet-ing In that land of light?

CHORUS.

Have we fought for Je-sus? Have we bat-tles won?
Can we say we've conquer'd? Sin-ner, what say you? Have we fought for Je-sus?
Sin-ner, are you read-y To go home to-night?

Are we brave and true? Are we sure of vic-t'ry? Sin-ner, what say you?

168 JESUS, LOVER OF MY SOUL.

(Tune, MARTYN.)

C. WESLEY.   SIMEON B. MARSH.

1. Je-sus, Lover of my soul, Let me to thy bo - som fly,... While the nearer
2. Other refuge have I none; Hangs my helpless soul on thee:.. Leave, O leave me
3. Thou, O Christ, art all I want; More than all in thee I find;.. Raise the fall-en
4. Plenteous grace with thee is found, Grace to cover all my sin:.. Let the heal-ing

waters roll, While the tempest still is high! Hide me, O my Saviour, hide, Till the
not a-lone, Still support and comfort me: All my trust on thee is stayed, All my
cheer the faint, Heal the sick, and lead the blind. Just and ho-ly is thy name, I am
streams abound: Make and keep me pure within. Thou of life the fountain art, Free-ly

storm of life is past; Safe in-to the heaven guide, O receive my soul at last!
help from thee I bring; Cover my defenceless head With the shadow of thy wing!
all un-right-eous-ness: False and full of sin I am, Thou art full of truth and grace.
let me take of thee: Spring thou up within my heart, Rise to all e-ter-ni-ty.

169 THE BLESSED TRINITY.

S. V. R. F.   STEPHEN V. R. FORD.

Glo-ry to the Fa-ther, Glo-ry to the Son, Glo-ry to the Spir-it, Blessed Three in One.

170   I SHALL SEE HIM BY AND BY.

J. F.

JOSEPH FLETCHER.

1. Je - sus reigns in heav'n a - bove, I shall see him by and by;
2. Christ, my Sav - iour, lead - eth me, I shall see him by and by;
3. If I serve him here be - low, I shall see him by and by;
4. Soon a home in heav'n I'll gain, I shall see him by and by;

In the land of light and love, I shall see him by and by.
He will give me vic - to - ry. I shall see him by and by.
Thro' the grace he doth be - stow, I shall see him by and by.
And with him for - ev - er reign, I shall see him by and by.

REFRAIN.

Glo - ry to his bless - ed name, He is ev - er - more the same;

He will guide me with his eye, I shall see him by and by.

A. C. F.

GUIDE ME.

REV. A. C. FERGUSON.

1. Dear Je-sus, my Lord, thy face I would see 'Mid the darkness and storm lest I stray;
2. Dear Je-sus, my Lord, thy voice I would hear When the tempest is raging a - round;
3. Dear Jesus, my Lord, my hands wilt thou hold When I pass thro' the Jordan's cold flood;

But I know full well wher - e'er my lot be, Thou wilt guide me by night and by day.
If its love-tones come thro' the blast to my ear, Peace will follow its sweet thrilling sound.
Till I safe-ly reach the dear Shepherd's fold To a - bide in the cit- y of God.

REFRAIN.

Guide me, Saviour, 'mid all sor-row; Guide me thro' each thorn-laced way;

Guide me this day and to - mor-row, Hear, O hear me when I pray.

"And, behold, the glory of the God of Israel came from the way of the east: . . . and the earth shined with his glory."—Ezek. 43. 2.

MARY A. LATHBURY.   STEPHEN V. R. FORD.

1. Wake! Christian, wake! the day is at the dawn-ing, Light aft - er night is
2. Rise! Christian, rise! if self be yet thy pris - on, See Je-sus' tomb—thou
3. Come! Christian, come! thy Lord has gone be - fore thee, Rough was the way of
4. Sing! Christian, sing! and fol - low him still sing-ing, Dark was the night, but

break-ing in the skies; Morn on the heights, and in the val-leys morning,
wilt not find him there, An - gels are telling the message, "he is ris - en!"
pain thro' which he passed; Fierce was the fight of sin thro' which he bore thee
see—thy light is come; Life out of death, and day from darkness bringing,

REFRAIN.

Fills earth and heav'n with joy, and calls, "A - rise!"
Rise from thy-self, and in his king-dom share.
To share his con-quest o - ver death at last.   Morn-ing of East - er!
Sing, for he leads his pil - grim peo - ple home!

morning of light! Shine on our darkness and chase a - way the night! Morning of

East-er! morn-ing of light! Shine on our darkness, and chase a - way the night.

173 SPEAK, O LORD, THY CHILD WILL HEAR THEE.

J. E. RANKIN, D.D.

ROBERT PAYSON.

1. Speak, O Lord, thy child will hear thee, Well I know my Fa - ther's voice;
2. Speak, O Lord, thy child will hear thee, Nev - er let me lose thy word;
3. Speak, O Lord, thy child will hear thee, Speak to me in ten - der tone;
4. Speed, O Lord, thy child will hear thee, Though the stars fall from their place,

I am hap - py to be near thee, In thy pre - sence I re - joice.
All thy voic - es more en - dear thee, Be no sin - gle one un - heard.
Though I love thee, I should fear thee, Wert thou not in Christ made known.
Though the an - gels shin - ing on thee, Lose the glo - ry of thy face.

In the world's that wheel a - bove me, In the flowr's strewn at my feet,
In the might - y, roll - ing thun - der, In the great ma - jes - tic sea,
When my heart for sin is brok - en, Ah the word thou hast for me!
That one word which thou hast spok-en, That one word there sealed in blood.

In the eyes of those that love me, I can hear thy ac - cents sweet.
Wak-ing in me awe and won - der, I can hear thy word to me.
In the u - ni - verse un - spo - ken, Save a - lone on cal - va - ry!
Nev - er, nev - er can be brok - en, God will make the com - pact good!

174   IN THE HOLLOW OF GOD'S HAND.

E. D. MUND.

E. S. LORENZ.

1. I am safe, what-ev-er may be-tide me; I am safe, who-ev-er may de-
2. What tho' fierce the stormy blasts roar round me; What tho' sore life's trials oft con-
3. Ev - er - last-ing arms of love en - fold me; Words of peace the voice divine has

ride me; I am safe, as long as I con-fide me In the hol-low of God's hand.
found me; I am safe, for naught of ill can wound me In the hol-low of God's hand.
told me; I am safe, while God himself doth hold me In the hol-low of God's hand.

Chorus.

In the hol-low, hol-low of his hand! In the

In the hol-low, in the hol-low of his hand!

hol-low, hol-low of his hand! I am

In the hol-low, in the hol-low of his hand!

safe while God him-self doth hold me In the hol-low of his hand.

Copyright, 1900, by E. S. Lorenz. By per.

O GLORY, HE SAVES EVEN ME.

REV. H. J. ZELLEY.

G. H. COOK.

1. My heart is thrilling with rap - ture, For Je - sus now is my Sav - iour;
2. When I was lost, Je - sus found me, He par - dons, cleanses and keeps me;
3. And now I'm con-stant-ly sing - ing, As in the light I am walk - ing;

He took my sin and my sor - row, And par-don-ing grace did be - stow.
From him no more will I wan - der, I tru - ly his serv-ice pre - fer.
My heart is flood- ed with sun-shine, This wonder - ful Je - sus is mine.

CHORUS.

O glo - ry, O glo - ry, I know that Je - sus now saves
glo-ry, he saves, O glo - ry, he saves, I know that Je - sus now saves e-ven

me; He saves me, he saves me, O glo - ry, he saves e - ven me.
me; He saves e-ven me, he saves e-ven me, e - ven me.

Then help me sing my song of praise To him who wondrously saves me; My

sweet-est song to him I'll raise, For he so wondrous-ly saves me.

176   JUST AS I AM.

(Tune: WOODWORTH.)

CHARLOTTE ELLIOTT.   W. B. BRADBURY, 1849.

1. Just as I am, with-out one plea, But that thy blood was shed for me,
2. Just as I am, and wait-ing not To rid my soul of one dark blot,
3. Just as I am, tho' tossed a-bout With many a con-flict, many a doubt,
4. Just as I am,—poor, wretched, blind; Sight, riches, healing of the mind,

And that thou bidd'st me come to thee, O Lamb of God, I come! I come!
To thee whose blood can cleanse each spot, O Lamb of God, I come! I come!
Fight-ings with-in, and fears without, O Lamb of God, I come! I come!
Yea, all I need, in thee to find, O Lamb of God, I come! I come!

5 Just as I am—thou wilt receive,
Wilt welcome, pardon, cleanse, relieve;
Because thy promise I believe;
O Lamb of God, I come! I come!

6 Just as I am—thy love unknown
Hath broken every barrier down;
Now, to be thine, yea, thine alone,
O Lamb of God, I come! I come!

A LITTLE TALK WITH JESUS.

ANON.   ARRANGED.

1. Tho' dark the night and clouds look black, And storm-y o - ver - head, And
2. When those who once were dearest friends Be - gin to per - se - cute, And
3. And thus, by fre-quent lit - tle talk,s I gain the vic - to - ry, And

trials of al - most ev - 'ry kind A - cross my path are spread; How
those who once pro-fessed to love Have si - lent grown and mute; I
march a - long with cheer-ful song, En - joy - ing lib - er - ty; With

soon I con - quer all, As to the Lord I call,— A lit - tle talk with
tell him all my grief, He quick-ly sends re - lief,— A lit - tle talk with
Je - sus as my friend, I'll prove un - til the end, A lit - tle talk with

D.S.—trials of ev - 'ry kind, Praise God, I al - ways find,— A lit - tle talk with

FINE.   CHORUS.

Je-sus makes it right, all right. A lit - tle talk with Je - sus makes it

Je - sus makes it right, all right.

D.S.

right, all right, A lit - tle talk with Je - sus makes it right, all right; In

A PRESENT VICTORY.

REV. H. J. ZELLEY.

G. H. COOK.

1. Pur - sued by Sa - tan, sin and death, No ref - uge could I see; But
2. I heard his voice, and felt his hand, Yet still I was not free, But
3. Temp-ta - tions great I oft - en meet, But to the Sav - iour flee; And
4. O hal - le - lu - jah, praise the Lord! I walk in lib - er - ty; I'm

Je - sus heard my pray'r and gave A pres - ent vic - to - ry.
when I gave up all, I found A pres - ent vic - to - ry.
thro' his grace I al - ways find A pres - ent vic - to - ry.
dead to self and Je - sus gives A pres - ent vic - to - ry.

CHORUS.

O glo - ry, glo - ry to his name! The blood now reach - es me, And,

1st. time.
2nd. time.

by its pow'r, I have to - day A pres-ent vic - to - ry, pres - ent vic-to - ry.

177

12

BEYOND.

MARIAN FROELICH.

G. FROELICH.

1. Be - yond the hills far, far a - way, The heav'n-ly fields my soul en - tice;
2. Tho' wea - ry, oft I onward press With courage toward the promised goal;
3. By faith I scale the heights a - far And leave the realms of night be - low,

And voic - es oft - en hith - er stray That ech - o songs of Par - a - dise:
I sink not 'neath the world's distress, Nor faint, since love sustains my soul:
For on be - yond the eve - ning star The sun of heaven beams, I know:

I hear the harpers sweep their strings, Their matchless strains my soul entrance;
And so, with Je - sus at my side, And un - der mine his arms of grace,
And while toward Pisgah's heights I climb, Tho' but a gleam to guide is giv'n,

While hope her cheer-ing message brings, "Look up! look up! nor earthward glance."
I jour - ney on, what-e'er be - tide, Nor fal - ter in the heavenly race.
Faith sings the rapt'rous song, "Sometime Thy voice shall join the choir of heav'n."

CHORUS.

Be - yond, Be - yond, And toward the light I'll climb,

Be - yond Be - yond I'll climb,

I'll gain the heights of bliss, of bliss some time.

I'll gain the heights some time.

180   JESUS, HOLD ME.

A. C. F.   REV. A. C. FERGUSON.

1. Je - sus, hold me when I'm fail - ing, 'Mid the storm's fierce surges wail - ing,
2. In my path there rears a mountain, Let me drink of thy peace-fount-ain;
3. Earthly ties and hu - man powers Fade and die, like sum - mer flow - ers,

Let me have thy will re - vealed; In the dark e - vents so try - ing,
Stay thou by me through the night; Anx-ious cares let me not bor - row;
But our Lord o'er all doth reign; He will bring us life e - ter - nal,

When heart-hopes are crushed and sigh-ing, Keep thou o'er me thy strong shield.
If my cup o'er-flow with sor - row, Je - sus, strength give by thy might.
Joys and sweet loves ev - er ver - nal, Soon he'll come for us a - gain.

179

181

TRUSTING IN JESUS ALONE.

L. E. JONES.

P. P. BILHORN.

1. Trusting in Je-sus, O why should I fear! Trusting in Je-sus when
2. Trusting in Je-sus who suf-fered for me, I have found mer-cy and
3. Haste thee, O Christian, no time for de-lay; Je-sus is call-ing for
4. Aft-er our work for the Mas-ter is o'er, Sweetly we'll rest on the

dan - ger is near; For my trans-gres-sions his blood doth a - tone,
par - don so free; He will keep safe - ly his loved and his own,
reap - ers to - day; Do not stand i - dle, the work must be done;
ev - er-green shore; There we shall reap from the seed we have sown,

CHORUS.

Trust-ing in Je - sus for - ev - er a - lone.
There is no oth - er but Je - sus a - lone.
Take for thy mot - to "Trust Je - sus a - lone."
Hap - py for - ev - er with Je - sus a - lone.

Trust - - ing in
Trusting in Je - sus, in

Je - - - sus, he............ can a - tone;............
Je - sus a - lone, Trust-ing in Je - sus, His blood can a - tone;

Trust - - ing in Je - - sus, Trusting in Je - sus a - lone.....
Trust-ing in Je - sus, his blood can a - tone, Trust-ing in Je - sus a - lone, a - lone.

Copyright, 1893, by P. P. Bilhorn. Used by per.

180

SOFTLY AND TENDERLY.

"Come unto me."—Matt. 11. 28.

W. L. T.

WILL L. THOMPSON.

Slow.

1. Soft - ly and ten-der - ly Je - sus is call-ing, Call-ing for you and for me;
2. Why should we tarry when Je - sus is pleading, Pleading for you and for me?
3. Time is now fleeting, the moments are passing, Passing from you and from me:
4. O for the won-der-ful love he has promis'd, Promis'd for you and for me;

See, on the por-tals he's wait-ing and watching, Watching for you and for me.
Why should we linger and heed not his mer-cies, Mer-cies for you and for me?
Shadows are gath-er-ing, death-beds are coming, Com-ing for you and for me.
Tho' we have sinned he has mer-cy and par-don, Par-don for you and for me.

CHORUS. *m*

Cres.

Come home,... Come home,... Ye who are wea-ry, come home,...

Come home, Come home,

p

rit.

p

Earn-est-ly, ten-der-ly, Je - sus is call-ing, Calling, O sinner, come home!

183 THE BEST FRIEND IS JESUS.

P. B.

P. BILHORN. By per.

Duet. Sop. (or Ten.) & Alto.

1. O the best friend to have is Je - sus, When the cares of life up-
2. What a friend I have found in Je - sus! Peace and com - fort to my
3. Tho' I pass thro' the night of sor - row, And the chil - ly waves of
4. When at last to our home we gath - er, With the loved ones who have

on you roll; He will heal the wound-ed heart, He will
soul he brings; Lean - ing on his might - y arm, I will
Jor - dan roll, Nev - er need I shrink or fear, For my
gone be - fore, We will sing up - on the shore, Prais - ing

strength and grace im - part; O the best friend to have is Je - sus.
fear no ill or harm; O the best friend to have is Je - sus.
Sav - iour is so near; O the best friend to have is Je - sus.
him for ev - er - more; O the best friend to have is Je - sus.

182

Chorus.—*Spirited.*

The best friend to have is Je - - - sus, The best friend to have is
Je-sus ev - ery day,

Je - - - sus, He will help you when you fall, He will
Je - sus all the way,

hear you when you call; O the best friend to have is Je - sus.

184   **AND CAN I YET DELAY?**

(Tune: BOYLSTON.)

CHARLES WESLEY.   LOWELL MASON.

1. And can I yet de - lay My lit - tle all to give? To tear my soul from
2. Nay, but I yield, I yield; I can hold out no more: I sink, by dy - ing

earth a - way For Je - sus to re - ceive?
love compelled, And own thee conquer - or.

3 My one desire be this,
  Thy only love to know;
To seek and taste no other bliss,
  No other good below.

4 My life, my portion thou;
  Thou all-sufficient art:
My hope, my heavenly treasure, now
  Enter, and keep my heart.

185   NEARER, MY GOD, TO THEE.

MRS. SARAH F. ADAMS.   SCOTCH AIR.

1. Near-er, my God, to thee ! Near-er to thee, E'en tho' it be a cross That rais-eth me;
2. Tho' like a wan-der-er, The sun gone down, Darkness be o-ver me, My rest a stone,
3. There let the way ap-pear, Steps un-to heav'n; All that thou sendest me, In mer-cy giv'n;
4. Then, with my waking tho'ts Bright with thy praise, Out of my ston-y griefs Beth-el I'll raise;
5. Or if, on joy-ful wing Cleaving the sky, Sun, moon and stars forgot, Upward I fly,

Still all my song shall be, Nearer, my God, to thee, Nearer, my God, to thee. Near-er to thee !
Yet in my dreams I'd be, Nearer, my God, to thee, Nearer, my God, to thee. Near-er to thee !
An-gels to beck-on me Nearer, my God, to thee, Nearer, my God, to thee. Near-er to thee !
So by my woes to be Nearer, my God, to thee, Nearer, my God, to thee. Near-er to thee !
Still all my song shall be, Nearer, my God, to thee, Nearer, my God, to thee. Near-er to thee !

186   GUIDE ME, O THOU GREAT JEHOVAH.
(Tune: ZION.)

WILLIAM WILLIAMS.   THOMAS HASTINGS.

1. Guide me, O thou great Je-ho-vah, Pil-grim thro' this bar-ren land; I am
2. O-pen now the crys-tal fount-ain, Whence the healing wa-ters flow; Let the
3. When I tread the verge of Jor-dan, Bid my anxious fears sub-side; Bear me

weak, but thou art might-y; Hold me with thy pow'r-ful hand; Bread of heav-en,
fier-y, cloud-y pil-lar Lead me all the jour-ney through; Strong De-liv-'rer,
thro' the swelling cur-rent; Land me safe on Ca-naan's side; Songs of prais-es

Feed me till I want no more. Bread of heav-en, Feed me till I want no more.
Be thou still my strength and shield. Strong De-liv-'rer, Be thou still my strength and shield.
I will ev-er give to thee. Songs of prais-es I will ev-er give to thee.

DEPTH OF MERCY.

CHARLES WESLEY.   JACQUES BLUMENTHAL, arr. by H. P. M.

1. Depth of mer-cy! can there be Mer-cy still re-served for me? Can my God his
2. Kin-dled his re-lent-ings are; Me he now de-lights to spare; Cries, "How shall I

wrath for-bear,—Me the chief of sin-ners, spare? I have long with-stood his grace; Long pro-
give thee up?" Lets the lift-ed thun-der drop. There for me the Sav-iour stands, Shows his

voked him to his face; Would not heark-en to his calls; Griev'd him by a thousand falls.
wounds and spreads his hands; God is love! I know, I feel; Je-sus weeps, and loves me still.

FOREVER HERE MY REST SHALL BE.

(Tune: AVON.)

CHARLES WESLEY.   HUGH WILSON.

1. For-ev-er here my rest shall be, Close to thy bleed-ing side;
2. My dy-ing Sav-iour, and my God, Fount-ain for guilt and sin,
3. Wash me, and make me thus thine own; Wash me, and mine thou art;
4. Th'a-tone-ment of thy blood ap-ply, Till faith to sight im-prove:

This all my hope, and all my plea, "For me the Sav-iour died."
Sprin-kle me ev-er with thy blood, And cleanse and keep me clean.
Wash me, but not my feet a-lone, My hands, my head, my heart.
Till hope in full fru-i-tion die, And all my soul be love.

189 O HAPPY DAY.
(Tune, HAPPY DAY.)

PHILIP DODDRIDGE, 1740.

1. O hap-py day that fixed my choice On thee, my Sav-iour and my God! Well may this
2. O hap-py bond, that seals my vows To him who mer-its all my love! Let cheer-ful
3. 'Tis done, the great trans-ac-tion's done; I am my Lord's, and he is mine; He drew me,
4. Now rest my long-di-vid-ed heart; Fixed on this bliss-ful cen-ter, rest, Nor ev-er

S. CHORUS.

glow-ing heart re-joice, And tell its rap-tures all a-broad.)
an-thems fill his house, While to that sa-cred shrine I move.   ) Hap-py day, hap-py day, When Je-sus
and I fol-lowed on, Charm'd to con-fess the voice di-vine. D.S.—
from thy Lord de-part, With him of ev-ery good possessed.) Hap-py day, hap-py day, When Je-sus

FINE.   D.S.

washed my sins a-way; He taught me how to watch and pray, And live re-joic-ing ev-ery day:
washed my sins a-way.

190 TELL IT TO JESUS.

ARR. BY WILLIAM JOHNSON.   J. B. O. CLEMM.

1 Brok-en in spir-it And la-den with care, Sweet is thy ref-uge, Find it in pray'r,
2. Art thou af-flict-ed, And sigh-ing to know Why the dear Father Should chasten thee so?
3 Art thou re-call-ing The years that have fled, Weep-ing in sor-row, Mourning the dead!
4. Bear thy af-flic-tion, What-ev-er it be, Je-sus, thy Sav-iour, Bore it for thee.

REFRAIN.

Tell it to Je-sus, Tell it to Je-sus, Tell it to Je-sus, He will give peace.

191 **WHEN I SURVEY THE WONDROUS CROSS.**

(Tune, ZEPHYR.)

ISAAC WATTS.   WILLIAM B. BRADBURY.

1. When I sur-vey the won-drous cross, On which the Prince of glo-ry died,
2. For-bid it, Lord, that I should boast, Save in the death of Christ, my God;
3. See, from his head, his hands, his feet, Sor-row and love flow min-gled down:
4. Were the whole realm of na-ture mine, That were a pres-ent far too small;

My rich-est gain I count but loss, And pour con-tempt on all my pride.
All the vain things that charm me most, I sac-ri-fice them to his blood.
Did e'er such love and sor-row meet, Or thorns com-pose so rich a crown.
Love so a-maz-ing, so di-vine, De-mands my soul, my life, my all.

192 **COME, YE DISCONSOLATE.**

THOMAS MOORE, alt., and THOMAS HASTINGS.   SAMUEL WEBBE.

1. Come, ye dis-con-so-late, wher-e'er ye lan-guish; Come to the mer-cy-seat, fer-vent-ly kneel;
2. Joy of the des-o-late, light of the stray-ing, Hope of the pen-i-tent, fade-less and pure.
3. Here see the bread of life; see wa-ters flow-ing Forth from the throne of God, pure from a-bove;

Here bring your wounded hearts, here tell your anguish; Earth has no sorrow that Heav'n cannot heal.
Here speaks the Comforter, ten-der-ly say-ing, "Earth has no sorrow that Heav'n cannot cure."
Come to the feast of love; come, ev-er know-ing Earth has no sorrow but Heav'n can re-move.

193 **MY COUNTRY! 'TIS OF THEE.**

SAMUEL F. SMITH.   HENRY CAREY, ad. from DR. JOHN BULL.

1. My coun-try! 'tis of thee, Sweet land of lib-er-ty, Of thee I sing: Land where my
2. My na-tive coun-try, thee, Land of the no-ble, free. Thy name I love; I love thy
3. Let mu-sic swell the breeze, And ring from all the trees Sweet freedom's song: Let mor-tal
4. Our fa-ther's God! to thee, Au-thor of lib-er-ty, To thee we sing: Long may our

MY COUNTRY! 'TIS OF THEE.—*Continued.*

fathers died! Land of the pilgrims' pride! From ev - ery mount-ain side Let free-dom ring!
rocks and rills, Thy woods and tem-pled hills; My heart with rap - ture thrills Like that a - bove.
tongues awake; Let all that breathe partake; Let rocks their si - lence break, The sound pro - long.
land be bright With freedom's ho - ly light; Pro - tect us by thy might, Great God, our King'

194   COME, SAID JESUS' SACRED VOICE.
(Tune, HORTON.)

MRS. ANNA L. BARBAULD.   XAVIER SCHNYDER.

1. Come, said Je - sus' sa - cred voice,   Come, and make my   paths your choice;
2. Thou who, house - less, sole, for - lorn,   Long hast borne the proud world's scorn,
3. Ye, who, tossed on beds of pain,   Seek for ease, but seek in vain;
4. Hith - er come, for here is found   Balm that flows for ev - ery wound.

I will guide you to your home;   Wea - ry pil - grim, hith - er come.
Long hast roamed the bar - ren waste, Wea - ry pil - grim, hith - er haste.
Ye, by fierce - er an - guish torn, In re - morse for guilt who mourn;
Peace that ev - er shall en - dure, Rest e - ter - nal, sa - cred, sure.

195   BLEST BE THE TIE THAT BINDS.
(Tune, DENNIS).

JOHN FAWCETT.   HANS GEORGE NAEGELI.

1. Blest be the tie that binds   Our hearts in Chris - tian love;
2. Be - fore our Fa - ther's throne, We pour our ar - dent pray'rs;
3. We share our mu - tual woes,   Our mu - tual bur - dens bear;
4. When we a - sun - der part,   It gives us in - ward pain:

The fel - low - ship of kin - dred minds Is like to that a - bove.
Our fears, our hopes, our aims are one, Our com - forts and our cares.
And oft - en for each oth - er flows The sym - pa - thiz - ing tear.
But we shall still be joined in heart, And hope to meet a - gain.

188

196 SAFELY THROUGH ANOTHER WEEK.

(Tune, SABBATH MORN.)

J. NEWTON.   L. M.

1. Safe-ly thro' an-oth-er week, God has brought us on our way; Let us now a blessing
2. While we pray for pardoning grace, Thro' the dear Re-deem-er's name, Show thy rec-on-cil-ed
3. Here we come thy name to praise; May we feel thy presence near: May thy glo-ry meet our

seek, Wait-ing in his courts to-day: Day of all the week the best, Em-blem
face, Take a-way our sin and shame; From our world-ly cares set free, May we
eyes, While we in thy house ap-pear: Here af-ford us, Lord, a taste Of our

of e-ter-nal rest; Day of all the week the best, Em-blem of e-ter-nal rest.
rest this day in thee; From our world-ly cares set free, May we rest this day in thee.
ev-er-last-ing feast; Here af-ford us, Lord, a taste Of our ev-er-last-ing feast.

197 FROM ALL THAT DWELL BELOW THE SKIES.

(Tune, DUKE STREET.)

I. WATTS.   JOHN HATTON.

1. From all that dwell be-low the skies, Let the Cre-a-tor's praise a-rise;
2. E-ter-nal are thy mer-cies, Lord; E-ter-nal truth at-tends thy word:
3. Your loft-y themes, ye mor-tals, bring; In songs of praise di-vine-ly sing;
4. In ev-ery land be-gin the song; To ev-ery land the strains be-long:

Let the Re-deem-er's name be sung, Thro' ev-ery land, by ev-ery tongue.
Thy praise shall sound from shore to shore, Till suns shall rise and set no more.
The great sal-va-tion loud pro-claim, And shout for joy the Sav-iour's name.
In cheer-ful sounds all voic-es raise, And fill the world with loud-est praise.

198   JESUS, SAVIOUR, PILOT ME.

REV. EDWARD HOPPER.   J. E. GOULD.

1. Je - sus, Sav - iour, pi - lot me, O - ver life's tempestuous sea; Unknown waves before me roll.
2. As a moth - er stills her child, Thou canst hush the o-cean wild; Boist'rous waves o-bey thy will,
3. When at last I near the shore, And the fear - ful breakers roar 'Twixt me and the peaceful rest.

Hid-ing rock and treach'rous shoal; Chart and compass come from thee; Je - sus, Sav-iour, pi - lot me.
When thou say'st to them "Be still!" Wondrous Sov'reign of the sea, Je - sus, Sav-iour, pi - lot me.
Then, while lean-ing on thy breast, May I hear thee say to me, "Fear not, I will pi - lot thee!"

199   I HEAR THY WELCOME VOICE.

L. H.   LEWIS HARTSOUGH.

1. I hear thy wel-come voice That calls me, Lord, to thee, For cleans-ing in thy
2. Tho' com - ing weak and vile, Thou dost my strength as-sure; Thou dost my vile-ness
3. 'Tis Je - sus calls me on To per - fect faith and love, To per - fect hope, and
4. 'Tis Je - sus who con-firms The bless - ed work with - in, By add - ing grace to
5. And be the wit - ness gives To loy - al hearts and free, That ev - ery prom-ise
6. All hail, a - ton-ing blood! All hail, re-deem-ing grace! All hail, the gift of

CHORUS.

pre - cious blood That flow'd on Cal - va - ry.
ful - ly cleanse, Till spot - less, all - and pure.
peace, and trust, For earth and heav'n a - bove.
wel - comed grace, Where reign'd the power of sin.
is ful - filled, If faith but brings the plea.
Christ, our Lord, Our strength and right - eous - ness!   } I am com - ing, Lord!

Com - ing now to thee! Wash me, cleanse me, in the blood That flow'd on Cal - va - ry.

200 SHALL WE FIND THEM AT THE PORTALS?

Rev. J. E. Rankin.

Prof. O. H. Evans, D.M.

The first part may be used as a Solo.

1. Will they meet us, cheer and greet us, Those we lov'd who've gone be - fore? Shall we find them at the por - tals, Find our beau - ti - fied im - mor - tals, When we reach that ra - diant shore!

2. Hearts are bro - ken for some to - ken, That they live and love us yet; And we ask, "Can those who've left us, Of love's look and tone be - reft us, Tho' in heav'n, can they for - get?"

3. And we oft - en, as days soft - en, And comes out the eve - ning star, Look - ing west - ward, sit and won - der, Whether when so far a - sun - der, They still think how dear they are!

4. Past yon por - tals, our im - mor - tals, Those who walk with him in white, Do they, 'mid their bliss, re - call us, Know they what e - vents be - fall us, Will our com - ing wake de - light!

rit.

191

CHORUS.
They will meet us, cheer and greet us,

They will meet us, cheer and greet us, Those we've lov'd who're

We shall find them at the por . . . tals.

gone be - fore; We shall find them at the por - tals, Find our

beau - ti - fied im - mor - tals, When we reach, when we reach that ra - diant shore.

201 MY FAITH LOOKS UP TO THEE.

(Tune, "OLIVET.")

RAY PALMER. LOWELL MASON.

1. My faith looks up to thee, Thou Lamb of Cal - va - ry, Sav - iour di - vine: Now hear me
2. May thy rich grace im - part Strength to my faint - ing heart, My zeal in - spire; As thou hast
3. While life's dark maze I tread, And griefs a - round me spread, Be thou my guide; Bid dark - ness
4. When ends life's transient dream, When death's cold, sullen stream Shall o'er me roll; Blest Sav - iour,

while I pray, Take all my guilt a - way, O let me from this day Be whol - ly thine.
died for me, O may my love to thee Pure, warm, and changeless be, — A liv - ing fire.
turn to - day, Wipe sorrow's tears a - way, Nor let me ev - er stray From thee a - side.
then, in love, Fear and dis - trust remove; O bear me safe a - bove, — A ransomed soul.

ONE SWEETLY SOLEMN THOUGHT.

MISS PHŒBE CARY.

PHILIP PHILLIPS, Mus. Doct.

1. One sweet-ly sol-emn thought Comes to me o'er and o'er; I'm near-er home to-
2. Near-er my Fa-ther's house, Where ma-ny man-sions be; Near-er the great white
3. Near-er the bound of life, Where burdens are laid down; Near-er to leave the
4. Be near me when my feet Are slip-ping o'er the brink, For I am near-er

day, to-day, Than I have been be-fore.
throne to-day, Near-er the crys-tal sea.
cross to-day, And near-er to the crown. } Near-er my home, Near-er my home,
home to-day, Per-haps, than now I think.

CHORUS.

Near-er my home to-day, to-day, Than I have been be-fore.

From *Song Sermons*, by per.

ABIDE WITH ME.
(Tune: "EVENTIDE.")

HENRY F. LYTE.

WM. HENRY MONK.

1. A-bide with me! Fast falls the e-ven-tide, The darkness deep-ens—Lord, with me a-bide!
2. Swift to its close ebbs out life's lit-tle day; Earth's joys grow dim, its glories pass a-way;
3. I need thy pres-ence ev-ery pass-ing hour; What but thy grace can foil the tempter's pow'r?
4. I fear no foe, with thee at hand to bless; Ills have no weight, and tears no bit-ter-ness;
5. Hold thou thy cross be-fore my clos-ing eyes; Shine thro' the gloom and point me to the skies;

When oth-er help-ers fail, and comforts flee, Help of the helpless, O a-bide with me!
Change and de-cay in all a-round I see; O thou, who changest not, a-bide with me!
Who, like thy-self, my guide and stay can be? Thro' cloud and sunshine, Lord, abide with me!
Where is death's sting? where, grave, thy victory? I triumph still, if thou a-bide with me!
Heaven's morning breaks, and earth's vain shadows flee; In life, in death, O Lord, a-bide with me!

I WILL SING FOR JESUS.

MRS. ELLEN M. H. GATES.   PHILIP PHILLIPS, Mus. Doct.

1. I will sing for Je - sus, With his blood he bought me; And all a - long my
2. Can there o - ver take me A - ny dark dis - as - ter, While I sing for
3. I will sing for Je - sus! His name a - lone pre - vail - ing, Shall be my sweet - est
4. Still I'll sing for Je - sus! Oh, how will I a - dore him, A - mong the cloud of

pil - grim way His lov - ing hand has brought me.
Je - sus, My bless - ed, bless - ed Mas - ter?
mu - sic, When heart and flesh are fail - ing. } Oh, help me sing for Je - sus, Help me
wit - ness - es, Who cast their crowns be - fore him.

CHORUS.

tell the sto - ry Of him who did re - deem us, The Lord of life and glo - ry.

205   COME, THOU ALMIGHTY KING.
                            (Tune: "ITALIAN HYMN.")

CHARLES WESLEY.   FELICE GIARDINI.

1. Come, thou al - might - y King, Help us thy name to sing, Help us to praise: Fa - ther all -
2. Come, thou in - car - nate Word, Gird on thy might - y sword, Our pray'r at - tend; Come, and thy
3. Come, ho - ly Com - fort - er, Thy sa - cred wit - ness bear In this glad hour; Thou who al -
4. To thee, great One and Three, E - ter - nal prais - es be, Hence ev - er - more: Thy sovereign

glo - ri - ous, O'er all vic - to - ri - ous, Come, and reign o - ver us, An - cient of days!
peo - ple bless, And give thy word suc - cess: Spir - it of ho - li - ness, On us de - scend!
might - y art, Now rule in ev - ery heart, And ne'er from us de - part, Spir - it of pow'r!
maj - es - ty May we in glo - ry see, And to e - ter - ni - ty Love and a - dore!

206 I HEARD THE VOICE OF JESUS SAY.

(Tune: INVITATION.)

H. BONAR.　　　　　　　　　　　　　　　　　　　LOUIS SPOHR.

1. I heard the voice of Je-sus say, "Come un-to me and rest; Lay down, thou wea-ry
2. I heard the voice of Je-sus say, "Be-hold, I free-ly give The liv-ing wa-ter;
3. I heard the voice of Je-sus say, "I am this dark world's Light; Look un-to me, thy

one, lay down Thy head up-on my breast!" I came to Je-sus as I was, Wea-
thirst-y one, Stoop down, and drink, and live!" I came to Je-sus, and I drank Of
morn shall rise And all thy day be bright!" I looked to Je-sus, and I found In

ry, and worn, and sad; I found in him a rest-ing-place, And he hath made me glad.
that life-giv-ing stream; My thirst was quench'd, my soul revived, And now I live in him.
him my Star, my Sun; And in that light of life I'll walk, Till all my jour-ney's done.

207　ALL PEOPLE THAT ON EARTH DO DWELL.

(Tune: OLD HUNDRED.)

WM. KETHE.　　　　　　　　　　　　　　　　　　LOUIS BOURGEOIS.

1. All peo-ple that on earth do dwell, Sing to the Lord with cheer-ful voice;
2. Know that the Lord is God in-deed, With-out our aid he did us make;
3. O en-ter then his gates with praise, Ap-proach with joy his courts un-to:
4. For why! the Lord our God is good, His mer-cy is for-ev-er sure;

Him serve with mirth, his praise forth tell, Come ye be-fore him, and re-joice.
We are his flock, he doth us feed, And for his sheep he doth us take.
Praise, laud, and bless his name al-ways, For it is seem-ly so to do.
His truth at all times firm-ly stood, And shall from age to age en-dure.

195

208

O DAY OF REST AND GLADNESS.

(Tune: MENDEBRAS.)

CHRISTOPHER WORDSWORTH.

GERMAN MELODY.

1. O day of rest and glad-ness, O day of joy and light, O balm of care and
2. On thee, at the cre - a - tion, The light first had its birth; On thee, for our sal -
3. New grac-es ev - er gain-ing From this our day of rest, We reach the rest re -

sad - ness, Most beau - ti - ful, most bright; On thee, the high and low - ly, Thro' a - ges
va - tion, Christ rose from depths of earth; On thee, our Lord, vic - to - rious, The Spir - it
main - ing To spir - its of the blest; To Ho - ly Ghost be prais-es, To Fa - ther,

joined in tune, Sing "Ho - ly, ho - ly, ho - ly," To the great God Tri - une.
sent from heav'n; And thus on thee, most glo - rious, A trip - le light was giv'n.
and to Son; The Church her voice up - rais - es To thee, blest Three in One.

209 COME, HOLY GHOST, OUR HEARTS INSPIRE.

(Tune: ST. MARTINS.)

CHARLES WESLEY.

WM. TANSUR.

1. Come, Ho - ly Ghost, our hearts in - spire; Let us thine in - fluence prove;
2. Come, Ho - ly Ghost, for moved by thee The proph - ets wrote and spoke;
3. Ex - pand thy wings, ce - les - tial Dove, Brood o'er our na - ture's night;
4. God, through him - self, we then shall know, If thou with - in us shine;

Source of the old pro - phet - ic fire, Fount-ain of life and love.
Un - lock the truth, thy - self the key; Un - seal the sa - cred book.
On our dis - or - dered spir - its move, And let there now be light.
And sound, with all thy saints be - low, The depths of love di - vine.

210

NETTLETON.

ROBERT ROBINSON.

JOHN WYETH, 1823.

1. Come, thou Fount of ev-ery bless-ing, Tune my heart to sing thy grace; Streams of mer-cy, nev-er
2. Here I'll raise mine Eb-en-e-zer; Hith-er by thy help I'm come; And I hope, by thy good
3. O to grace how great a debt-or Dai-ly I'm constrained to be! Let thy goodness, like a

ceas-ing, Call for songs of loud-est praise. Teach me some me-lo-dious son-net, Sung by
pleas-ure, Safe-ly to ar-rive at home. Je-sus sought me when a stranger, Wand'ring
fet-ter, Bind my wand'ring heart to thee: Prone to wan-der, Lord, I feel it, Prone to

flam-ing tongues a-bove; Praise the mount—I'm fixed up-on it—Mount of thy re-deem-ing love!
from the fold of God; He, to res-cue me from dan-ger, In-ter-posed his pre-cious blood.
leave the God I love: Here's my heart, O take and seal it; Seal it for thy courts a-bove.

211

NEW HAVEN.

ROBERT II., King of France. Tr. RAY PALMER.

THOMAS HASTINGS.

1. Come, Ho-ly Ghost, in love, Shed on us from a-bove Thine own bright ray! Di-vine-ly
2. Come, tend'rest Friend, and best, Our most delightful Guest, With soothing power: Rest which the
3. Come, all the faith-ful bliss; Let all who Christ con-fess His praise em-ploy: Give vir-tue's

good thou art; Thy sa-cred gifts im-part To glad-den each sad heart: O come to-day!
wea-ry know, Shade, 'mid the noon-tide glow, Peace when deep griefs o'er-flow, Cheer us, this hour!
rich re-ward; Vic-to-rious death ac-cord, And with our glo-rious Lord, E-ter-nal joy!

197

HOLY SPIRIT, FAITHFUL GUIDE.

M. M. WELLS.

MARCUS MORRIS WELLS.

1. Ho - ly Spir - it, faith - ful guide, Ev - er near the Christian's side; Gen - tly lead us
2. Ev - er pres - ent, tru - est Friend, Ev - er near thine aid to lend, Leave us not to
3. When our days of toil shall cease, Wait - ing still for sweet re - lease, Noth - ing left but

by the hand, Pil - grims in a des - ert land; Wea - ry souls for e'er re - joice, While they
doubt and fear, Grop - ing on in dark - ness drear, When the storms are rag - ing sore, Hearts grow
heav'n and pray'r, Wond'ring if our names were there; Wad - ing deep the dis - mal flood, Plead - ing

hear that sweet-est voice Whisp'ring soft - ly, wanderer come! Fol - low me, I'll guide thee home!
faint, and hopes give o'er, Whis - per soft - ly, wanderer come! Fol - low me, I'll guide thee home!
naught but Je - sus' blood! Whis - per soft - ly, wanderer come! Fol - low me, I'll guide thee home!

ROCK OF AGES, CLEFT FOR ME.
(Tune: TOPLADY.)

A. M. TOPLADY, alt.

THOMAS HASTINGS.

1. Rock of a - ges, cleft for me, Let me hide my - self in thee; Let the wa - ter and the blood,
2. Could my tears for - ev - er flow, Could my zeal no languor know, These for sin could not a - tone;
3. While I draw this fleeting breath, When my eyes shall close in death, When I rise to worlds unknown,

From thy wounded side which flowed, Be of sin the doub - le cure, Save from wrath and make me pure:
Thou must save, and thou a - lone: In my hand no price I bring; Simp - ly to thy cross I cling.
And be - hold thee on thy throne, Rock of a - ges, cleft for me, Let me hide my - self in thee.

HOW I LOVE JESUS.

FREDERICK WHITFIELD, 1859.　　　　　　　　　　AMERICAN SPIRITUAL.

1. There is a name I love to hear, I love to sing its worth; It sounds like
2. It tells me of a Saviour's love, Who died to set me free; It tells me
3. It tells me what my Fa-ther hath In store for ev-ery day, And, though I
4. It tells of One, whose lov-ing heart Can feel my deep-est woe, Who in each

mu-sic in mine ear—The sweetest name on earth
of his precious blood, The sin-ner's per-fect plea.　　Oh, how I love Je-sus,
tread a dark-some path, Yields sun-shine all the way.
sor-row bears a part, That none can bear be-low.

CHORUS.

Oh, how I love Je-sus, Oh, how I love Je-sus, Be-cause he first loved me.

HEAR MY CRY.

FANNY J. CROSBY.　　　　　　　　　　PHILIP PHILLIPS. By per.

1. Son of Da-vid, hear my cry! Saviour, do not pass me by; Touch these eyelids veiled in night,
2. Tho' the proud my voice would still, They may chide me if they will, Yet the more I'll pray for grace,
3. Tho' despised by all but thee, Then a blessing hast for me; Faith and pray'r can nev-er fail,
4. Glorious vis-ion! heavenly ray! All my gloom has passed a-way; Now my joy-ful eye doth see,

Turn their darkness in-to light, Son of Da-vid, hear my cry! Saviour, do not pass me by.
On-ly here shall be my place, Son of Da-vid, hear my cry! Saviour, do not pass me by;
Lord, with thee, I must prevail! Son of Da-vid, hear my cry! Saviour, do not pass me by.
And my soul still clings to thee; Thine the glo-ry ev-er-more, Mine to worship and a-dore.

216 SILENT NIGHT.

JOSEPH MOHR.

FRANZ GRUBER, 1818.

1. Si - lent night! Ho - ly night! All is calm, all is bright Round yon vir - gin
2. Si - lent night! Ho - ly night! Shep-herds quake at the sight! Glo - ries stream from

moth - er and Child! Ho - ly In - fant, so ten - der and mild, Sleep in heav - en - ly
heav - en a - far Heav - en - ly hosts sing Al - le - lu - ia, Christ, the Sav - iour is

peace, Sleep in heav - en - ly peace.
born! Christ, the Sav - iour is born!

3.

Silent night! Holy night!
Son of God, love's pure light
Radiant beams from thy holy face,
With the dawn of redeeming grace,
Jesus, Lord, at thy birth,
Jesus, Lord, at thy birth.

217 I DO BELIEVE.

CHARLES WESLEY.

1. Fa - ther, I stretch my hands to thee; No oth - er help I know?
2. What did thine on - ly Son en - dure, Be - fore I drew my breath?
3. O Je - sus, could I this be - lieve, I now should feel thy power;
4. Au - thor of faith! to thee I lift My wea - ry, long - ing eyes:

CHO.—I will be - lieve, I do be - lieve, That Je - sus died for me;

D. C. for CHO.

If thou with - draw thy - self from me, Ah! whith - er shall I go?
What pain, what la - bor, to se - cure My soul from end - less death!
And all my wants thou wouldst re - lieve, In this ac - cept - ed hour.
O, let me now re - ceive that gift,— My soul with - out it dies.
And thro' his blood, his pre - cious blood, I shall from sin be free.

200

218 CLEANSING FOUNTAIN.

WM. COWPER.   WESTERN MELODY.

1. There is   a fount-ain filled with blood,   Drawn from Immanuel's veins;   And sin-ners, plung'd be-
2. The dy - ing thief re-joiced to see   That fount-ain in   his   day;   And there may I, though
3. Thou dy - ing Lamb! thy pre-cious blood   Shall nev - er lose its power,   Till all   the ran-somed
4. E'er since, by faith, I saw the stream Thy flow-ing wounds sup-ply,   Re-deem-ing love has
5. Then in   a no - bler, sweet - er song, I'll sing thy power to save,   When this poor lisp-ing,

CHORUS.

neath that flood, Lose all their guilt - y   stains.
vile   as   he,   Wash all my sins a - way.
Church of God   Are saved, to sin   no   more, } Lose all their guilt - y   stains,   Lose
been   my theme, And shall be till I   die.
stamm'ring tongue, Lies si - lent in   the grave.

all their guilt - y stains; And sin-ners, plung'd be-neath that flood, Lose all their guilt - y   stains.

219 HAVE YOU HEARD?

S. A.   REV. SAMUEL ALMAN.

Adagio.

1. Have you heard the news proclaim'd, How the wand'rers are reclaim'd, And the blind, and halt, and maim'd,
2. Have you heard how Chris-tians go, In - to homes of want and woe, Just to let poor sin-ners know
3. Let your voic - es then pro-claim, In the haunts of sin and shame, Free for-give-ness in his name,

CHORUS.

Have a Friend in Je - sus?
What a Friend is Je - sus? } A Friend in need, a Friend in-deed, Have you this Friend in Je-sus?
Pre - cious name of Je - sus.

220

JOY TO THE WORLD.

(Tune: ANTIOCH.)

ISAAC WATTS.　　　　　　　　　　　　　　　Arr. from GEO. F. HANDEL.

1. Joy to the world! the Lord is come; Let earth re-ceive her King; Let
2. Joy to the world! the Sav-iour reigns; Let men their songs em-ploy; While
3. No more let sin and sor-row grow, Nor thorns in-fest the ground; He
4. He rules the world with truth and grace, And makes the na-tions prove The

ev-ery heart pre-pare him room, And heav'n and na-ture sing, And
fields and floods, rocks, hills, and plains, Re-peat the sound-ing joy, Re-
comes to make his bless-ings flow Far as the curse is found, Far
glo-ries of his right-cous-ness, And won-ders of his love, And

And heav'n, and heav'n and na-ture
Re-peat, etc.

heav'n and na-ture sing, And heav'n, and heav'n and na-ture sing.
peat the sound-ing joy, Re-peat, re-peat the sound-ing joy.
as the curse is found, Far as, far as the curse is found.
won-ders of his love, And wonders, and won-ders of his love.

sing, And heav'n and na-ture sing.

221

I'M A PILGRIM.

FINE.

1. I'm a pil-grim, and I'm a stran-ger: I can tar-ry, I can tar-ry but a night.
2. There the sun-beams are ev-er shin-ing, Oh, my long-ing heart, my long-ing heart is there.
3. Of that coun-try to which I'm go-ing, My Re-deem-er, my Re-deem-er is the light;

CHORUS.

I'm a pil-grim, and I'm a stran-ger: I can tar-ry, I can tar-ry but a night.

D.C. for CHO.

Do not de-tain me, for I am go-ing To where the streamlets are ev-er flow-ing.
Here in this coun-try, so dark and drear-y, I long have wan-dered for-lorn and wea-ry.
There is no sor-row, nor a-ny sigh-ing. Nor a-ny sin there, nor a-ny dy-ing.

TOPICAL INDEX.

INDEX.

TITLES AND FIRST LINES.

To facilitate the finding of Hymns the *Titles* are set in SMALL CAPS on the margin, and *First Lines* in Roman, slightly to the right. The names of old tunes, such as "Antioch" and "Austria," which are neither titles nor first lines, will be found among the first lines in Roman.

204

INDEX.

INDEX.

207

INDEX.

W

Y

Z